VIENNESE
CUISINE

VIENNESE CUISINE

—— .•. ——

THE NEW APPROACH

Peter Grunauer
Andreas Kisler

WITH
Donald Flanell Friedman

JOHN MURRAY

This revised edition first published 1989
by John Murray (Publishers) Ltd
50 Albemarle Street
London W1X 4BD

This book was first published in the United States of
America by Doubleday, New York 1987

British Library Cataloguing in Publication Data
Grunauer, Peter
Viennese cuisine: the new approach.
1. Food: Viennese dishes – Recipes
I. Title   II. Kisler, Andreas   III.
Flanell Friedman, Donald
641.59436'13

ISBN 0–7195–4604–4 (cased)
ISBN 0–7195–4608–7 (limp)

Typeset by Butler & Tanner
Printed and bound in Great Britain
by Butler & Tanner Frome and London

Contents

Preface

A PERFECT balance of delicacy and sensuousness of flavour characterises modern Viennese cooking. The refinement of this cuisine is the culmination of the long evolution of Viennese cooking, always multi-national in character. As the capital of the Habsburg empire, Vienna was the convergence point of an immense realm that extended from the Adriatic to the borders of Russia. Habsburgs governed not only the contemporary Eastern European nations of Hungary, Czechoslovakia, and parts of Yugoslavia and Romania, but also at various epochs during their six-hundred year reign, much of nothern Italy, Sicily, Sardinia, Spain, Flanders, Burgundy, Mexico, and Peru, among other areas. No fewer than sixteen languages were spoken in the empire before the outbreak of the First World War. Viennese cuisine naturally expressed and was enriched by the most varied influences.

Peter Grunauer's own background reflects this spirit of internationalism. He grew up in an environment in which food was a passionate interest. As soon as he was old enough to reach the tables, he waited on customers at his parents' popular restaurant in Vienna's Seventh District, which specialises in traditional Austrian cooking. Mr Grunauer, a skilled chef as well as a restaurateur, was trained on two continents, studying at the Hotel School in Vienna and at Cornell University in the United States. He has worked for many years with creative chef Andreas Kisler, trained at the restaurant of the Palais Schwarzenberg, citadel of elegant dining in Vienna, as well as at La Marée, one of the finest seafood restaurants in Paris. This cross-fertilisation of Austrian and French culinary ideas is also rooted in tradition. During the 1815 Congress of Vienna, Talleyrand brought a potent diplomatic weapon to Austria, the chef Marie-

Antoine Carême, who became the master of the *grand cuisine* of Europe. Like Brillat-Savarin, Andreas Kisler believes that 'the discovery of a new dish does more for the happiness of the human race than the discovery of a star.' Emphasising the freshest herbs and choicest ingredients, many of the recipes in this book are Mr Kisler's transformations and interpretations of the traditional. In 1985 he was the youngest of the ten chefs chosen to appear on the television programme 'The Master Chefs of New York.'

Peter Grunauer hopes to bring about a renaissance of Austrian cooking and to make a statement about fine dining. He strongly denies the identification of Austrian cooking with overly assertive peasant fare. He believes that contemporary Austrian cuisine must be true to its heritage by continuing to evolve, developing into the gourmet fare of today: food that is light, plentiful, and beautifully served, exciting to look at, enticing to the appetite. Peter Grunauer conceives of a meal as a feast for all the senses: beginning with the keynote of the first course, to awaken the palate, harmoniously developed through the main course, and culminating in one of the celestial desserts for which Vienna is justly famed. This new approach to cooking represents a culinary celebration of life's abundance, the profusion of its good things, and also of finesse.

Donald Flanell Friedman

Introduction

Gemütlichkeit could be said to be our Austrian attitude toward living. The word is difficult to translate literally, but implies a relaxed and knowledgeable enjoyment of all the pleasures of life. Cooking, basic and vital for survival, is an art form. A special dinner should be an event that lingers in memory, a source of delight to you and your guests.

It was several years ago that I first decided to write a book which, I hoped, would change ideas about Vinnese cooking. It is evident that we live in a health-conscious age. Chef Andreas Kisler and I believe that Austrian food need not be just the hearty fare enjoyable on a winter's day. Such dishes, of course, have an important place on the menu, and you will find recipes in our book for the best of the traditional favourites. There are times, however, when you will decide to serve food that is light without sacrificing flavour. We are convinced that our light versions of Viennese classics gain in flavour from the very delicacy of the sauces, made by reduction, without any flour or thickener, and the refinement with which we combine choice ingredients.

You will find that we have included many interesting and creative recipes for fish, one of the healthiest of protein sources. Before World War I, Austria had territory on the Adriatic and was supplied with a profusion of seafood. True to the spirit of the past, when fish markets flourished in Vienna, I have a great variety and quantity of fresh seafood flown to my New York restaurant daily from around the world.

Because of its lightness and subtlety, seafood makes an ideal first course. You may want to establish a sense of progression in your meal by complementing a fish or shell fish first dish with a main course such as our Rosy Lamb Fillets with Mint Sauce enhanced by an array of bright vegetables. Bear in mind while following our recipes that all tastes should maintain their integrity while combining to form a remarkable whole. The composite flavour of the dish must be that of the products used in making it. For this reason you should use only the best and freshest products available. Remember to let the time of year and availability of fine ingredients help you decide which recipes to choose. Why defeat your effort to prepare something special by using an inferior cut of meat or tinned or frozen produce?

A word about dessert, which is an integral part of dinner in Austria: Vienna is famous the world over for its coffee-houses and pastry-shops where you can sit for hours, sipping a wide variety of coffees and sampling sweets. Here we share our versions of the beloved pastries, in recipes in which the quantity of flour has often been reduced, enabling even the serious weight-watcher to indulge in the inimitable pleasure of a Viennese dessert. As an unusual ending to a special dinner, you might want to give your guests our Kapuziner Palatschinken, crêpes filled with warm chestnut purée and served with chocolate sauce, or our Topfenknödel, fluffy little curd cheese dumplings in a gleaming fruit sauce. You might decide to arrange small portions of several desserts on a plate – a tiny square of dark chocolate Sachertorte, contrasting with a creamy little dollop of mousse and a cloud of frozen Praline Parfait, the whole set off with refreshing crescents of melon.

I hope you will enjoy the blend of the traditional Austrian and international cuisine which my chef, Andreas Kisler, and I have developed. We wish you great pleasure in preparing and serving our recipes. You won't need to know any special techniques or culinary secrets. You need only be willing to relax and enjoy the process of cooking; I believe that there is no greater pleasure in life than preparing a wonderful meal for your guests and enjoying it in their company.

New York City   PETER GRUNAUER
July 1985

2

First Courses

BEAUTIFUL COLOURS and appealing presentation are essential for the first course, the moment of the meal that establishes a relaxed mood of conviviality, pleasurable surprise, and anticipation of the culinary adventure to follow.

In all of our first courses, flavours maintain their integrity and natural distinction. These dishes represent our style, a mixture of the traditional Viennese, variations on classic themes, and our own innovations. Healthy seafood abounds. Our seafood salads and terrines can be made a day in advance of your dinner party, and many of our starters can be served as main courses.

——··——

VIENNESE CHANTERELLES

FOR SIX PEOPLE

85 g (3 oz) butter
2 medium onions, finely diced
700 g (1½ lb) chanterelles, rinsed, dried on kitchen paper, and torn by hand into quarters
115 ml (scant ¼ pt) double cream
1 tablespoon fresh thyme, or to taste

6 eggs
½ bunch parsley (leaves only), rinsed, dried, and finely chopped
salt and freshly ground white pepper to taste

1 In a frying pan, heat 60 g (2 oz) of the butter, add the onions, and sauté for 5 minutes over high heat. Add the chanterelles and sauté for 5 more minutes.

2 Add the double dream to the frying pan, cover, and allow to simmer over low heat for about 5 minutes, until the chanterelles are tender.

3 Season with the thyme and salt and pepper to taste. Leave the frying pan uncovered and keep warm over low heat.

4 Meanwhile, in a separate pan, fry the eggs in the remaining butter. Drain on kitchen towels.

5 Arrange the chanterelles on six warm plates. Sprinkle with the chopped parsley and top each plate with a fried egg.

●The chanterelle, known for its egg-yolk-yellow colour and slightly peppery taste, is particularly prized in Viennese cuisine. This is a traditional recipe that you will find makes a delicious first course or light main dish. Try it with crusty black bread to soak up the rich mushroom cream. Our recommendation for an appropriate wine is Austrian Pinot Blanc by Klosterkeller Siegendorf or a good Mâcon Villages.

—— •.• ——

WARM DUCK SALAD WITH FRENCH BEANS

FOR SIX PEOPLE

1 duck, weighing about 2.3–2.7 kg (5–6 lb)
700 g (1½ lbs) French beans, tips removed
5 tablespoons olive oil
4 tablespoons sherry vinegar
4 mushroom caps, thinly sliced
4 shallots, peeled and thinly sliced
⅛ teaspoon fresh thyme
2 bayleaves
10 black peppercorns
salt and freshly ground white pepper to taste

1 Preheat the oven to 190°C/375°F/Gas 5.

2 Roast the duck for 2 hours, until golden brown. Remove the duck legs and breast. Set aside to cool. Reserve the rest of the duck for another recipe.

3 While the duck is roasting, bring 2 litres (3½ pts) of salted water to a boil in a large saucepan and add the beans. Boil for 4 to 5 minutes until cooked, but still crisp. Refresh in iced water to retain their bright colour, then drain.

4 In a glass bowl, combine the olive oil, half of the vinegar, the mushrooms, shallots, thyme, bay leaves, and peppercorns. Season with salt and pepper to taste, toss well, and set aside to marinate at room temperature for at least 1 hour.

5 Pour the remaining vinegar into a separate glass bowl. Season with salt and pepper to taste. Add the beans, toss well to coat, and set aside to marinate at room temperature for at least 1 hour.

6 Bone the duck legs, and carve them into thin slices. Cut the duck breast into strips.

7 To serve, drain the vegetables, and combine the two marinades. Arrange equal portions of vegetables on six individual plates. Cover with slices of duck meat and sprinkle the marinade over the top.

●This pairing of warm, savoury duck and crisp, cold French beans is a year-round favourite.

——— •••• ———

BREAST OF CHICKEN POACHED WITH HERBS

FOR SIX PEOPLE

1 egg yolk
1 teaspoon honey
2 tablespoons white vinegar
juice of 1 lemon
4 tablespoons grape-seed oil or olive oil
4 chicken breasts, with bones removed and reserved for making stock*
2 tablespoons each fresh tarragon, peppermint, basil, and rosemary coarsely chopped and mixed together
6 lettuce leaves
1 medium cantaloupe melon, cut lengthwise into halves, with seeds removed, cut from the peel, and cut lengthways into 1.25 cm ($\frac{1}{2}$") slices
salt and pepper to taste

1 Mix the egg yolk, honey, vinegar, and lemon juice in a bowl. When blended, season with salt and pepper to taste. Add the oil slowly, drop by drop, whisking gently until the dressing is thick and smooth. Set aside.

5

2 Place the bones from the chicken breasts in a saucepan and cover with 1 litre (generous 1½ pts) of water. Add all the herbs. Bring to a boil, immediately lower the heat, and simmer over low heat, uncovered, until the liquid is reduced to 425 ml (¾ pt).

3 Strain the stock through cheesecloth and then skim the fat from the top of the strained stock. Remove 2 tablespoons of the broth, allow to cool, and then stir into the prepared dressing.

4 Bring the remaining stock to the boil in a large frying pan. If you are using cube or tinned, add the herbs now to poach with the chicken. Add the chicken breasts, cover, and simmer over low heat for 6 to 8 minutes.

5 Remove the poached chicken from the broth and allow to cool. Cut the chicken into 2.5 cm (1″) cubes. Put six plates to chill.

6 Place a lettuce leaf on each chilled plate; cover with chicken cubes and garnish attractively with the melon slices. Pour the dressing over the tips of the melon slices and the chicken cubes and lettuce.

●This makes an enticing starter or a light main course. You need serve nothing more than good French bread and a well-chilled, fruity white wine. We recommend Sauvignon Blanc by Klosterkeller Siegendorf, or Napa Valley Chardonnay.

●If making the chicken stock is too time-consuming, you may substitute bouillon cubes dissolved in water or tinned chicken broth. Approximately 450 ml (scant pint) is needed.

——— • • • ———

SWEETBREADS AND FOIE GRAS ON SEASONAL SALAD

FOR SIX PEOPLE

450 g (1 lb) sweetbreads, repeatedly rinsed in running water, with lining and sinews removed, and then refreshed in iced water

flour for coating

450 g (1 lb) fresh or vacuum-packed foie gras (do not use tinned)

1 whole egg

4 tablespoons walnut oil, plus 3–4 tablespoons for sautéing

1 egg yolk

4 tablespoons sherry vinegar

fresh seasonal lettuce leaves

salt and freshly ground white pepper to taste

1 Cut the cleaned sweetbreads into twelve slices. Dip both sides of the sweetbread slices in the flour. Pat them to prevent the flour from becoming lumpy. Slice the foie gras also into twelve pieces, and flour.

2 Whisk the whole egg in a bowl and dip each floured slice of sweetbread in the egg. Dip the foie gras in flour only.

3 Heat 3 tablespoons of the walnut oil in a frying pan and sauté the sweetbreads and foie gras over medium heat until golden. You will probably need to do this in batches; add more walnut oil if necessary. Keep the cooked slices warm on a covered plate.

4 Meanwhile, mix the egg yolk and sherry vinegar in a bowl. Add the 4 tablespoons walnut oil, drop by drop, whisking continuously, until blended and creamy. Season with salt and white pepper to taste.

5 Arrange lettuce leaves in the centre of six plates. Drizzle the dressing on to the lettuce. Place two warm slices each of sweetbread and foie gras on the plates, surrounding the salad like the points of a compass.

●This uncomplicated dish is simple to prepare and a fine way to begin a winter meal.

—— •••• ——

SCALLOPS IN A VERMOUTH AND SAFFRON SAUCE

FOR SIX PEOPLE

oil for sautéing, preferably corn or sunflower

24 scallops, removed from their shells, sliced into halves

2 shallots, peeled and finely diced

4 tablespoons dry vermouth

225 ml (scant ½ pt) double cream

pinch of saffron

juice of 1 lemon

2 pink grapefruits, peeled and sectioned

salt and freshly ground white pepper to taste

1 In a frying pan, heat approximately 2 tablespoons of oil to sizzling and sauté the scallops briefly, not more than 2 minutes. Remove the scallops and place in a covered dish to keep warm.

2 Pour 1 tablespoon fresh oil into the frying pan and sauté the shallots until transparent.

3 Add the vermouth and reduce over medium-high heat until 2 tablespoons are left.

4 Add the cream and saffron. Reduce by half over low heat to a creamy consistency. Season with the lemon juice and with salt and pepper to taste.

5 Strain the sauce through a fine sieve and discard the shallots.

6 Pour the sauce onto six warm plates. Arrange the scallops in a cross pattern on each plate. Place one grapefruit section between each two arms of the cross.

——— ••• ———

SALMON AND SCALLOP SALAD

FOR SIX PEOPLE

8 tablespoons dry white wine
8 tablespoons dry vermouth
2 bay leaves
6 peppercorns
225 g (8 oz) fresh salmon, cut
    into 1.25 cm ($\frac{1}{2}$") cubes
6 scallops, removed from their
    shells
450 g (1 lb) small green beans,
    rinsed, with both tips
    snapped off

6 shallots, peeled and finely
    sliced
2 spring onions (both white and
    green parts), cut into pieces
2 egg yolks
1 teaspoon tarragon vinegar
8 tablespoons good olive oil
salt and freshly ground white
    pepper to taste

1 Bring the wine, vermouth, 225 ml (scant $\frac{1}{2}$ pint) of water, the bay leaves, and peppercorns to the boil in a saucepan. Add the salmon cubes and scallops, then immediately lower the heat and simmer 3 to 4 minutes. (Never allow fish to boil, for over-cooking will ruin its flavour.)

2 Remove the seafood from the stock and set aside to cool. Discard the bay leaves, and peppercorns. Leave the stock on very low heat.

3 Cook the beans 6 to 8 minutes in the simmering fish stock. The beans should remain quite crisp.

4 Remove the beans and set the stock aside to cool. Refresh the beans in a bowl of iced water and drain.

5 When the stock is cool, add the beans, shallots, and spring onions and refrigerate.

6 Mix the egg yolks and vinegar in a bowl. Drop by drop, add the olive oil, whisking the entire time, until the dressing thickens to the consistency of mayonnaise.

7 Thin the dressing by stirring in 3 tablespoons of the chilled fish stock. Season with salt and pepper to taste.

8 To serve, remove the bean mixture from the stock. Place the mixture in a bowl with the poached salmon, add the salad dressing, and mix gently. Distribute among six plates and garnish each with a scallop.

●This summery cool seafood salad, which is also a fine main dish, can be made in a day in advance of your dinner party and refrigerated.

———— •·• ————

SCALLOP AND CRAYFISH SALAD, SERVED WITH CANTALOUPE MELON AND PINK GRAPEFRUIT SECTIONS

FOR SIX PEOPLE

12 scallops, removed from their shells
dry white wine for poaching
12 live crayfish (or 12 large prawns)
3 egg yolks
1 tablespoon tarragon vinegar
2 tablespoons walnut oil
425 ml (¾ pt) soured cream
2 peeled and cored Granny Smith apples, cut into 2.5 cm (1″) cubes
15 g (½ oz) walnuts, chopped

2 tablespoons finely chopped fresh tarragon (1 tablespoon dried tarragon may be used if necessary)
6 medium tomatoes, peeled, with seeds removed, cut into 2.5 cm (1″) cubes
salt and freshly ground white pepper to taste
juice of 1 lemon (about)
2 pink grapefruits
1 small cantaloupe melon

1 Place the scallops in a frying pan and add enough wine to cover. Heat over a moderate flame until the scallops are lightly poached, about 7 to 8 minutes. They should remain tender. Remove the scallops and set aside, leaving the stock in the pan.

2 Boil the live crayfish in the scallop stock for 1 minute. Remove the crayfish and cool them in ice water. Break the tails in half carefully and remove the meat. Place the crayfish meat in the bowl with the scallops and set aside.

3 In a bowl, mix together the egg yolks and tarragon vinegar. Add the walnut oil, drop by drop, whisking constantly, until it reaches a mayonnaise consistency. Stir in the soured cream.

If the dressing is too thick, add some of the fish stock, a little at a time.

4 Add the apples, walnuts, tarragon, and tomatoes. Stir. Mix the crayfish and scallops into the dressing. Add salt, pepper, and lemon juice to taste. Refrigerate.

5 Peel the grapefruits and separate and peel the segments. Peel the melon, cut in half, remove the seeds, and slice thinly. Arrange the fruit attractively on one side of six chilled plates, and place the seafood salad in the centre.

—— ·•· ——

RAGOUT OF CRAYFISH TAILS, CHANTERELLES, AND OYSTERS

FOR SIX PEOPLE

36 live crayfish, boiled in salted water for 2 minutes, then refreshed in iced water
dry white wine for cooking the oysters
12 Belon oysters, rinsed
225 ml (scant ½ pt) double cream
3 tablespoons oil for sautéing
4 shallots, peeled and finely sliced

100 g (3 oz) chanterelles, rinsed, patted dry with paper towels, and torn in half
2 tablespoons cognac
½ teaspoon fresh thyme
1 clove garlic, peeled
juice of 1 lemon
salt and freshly ground white pepper to taste

1 Remove the meat from the boiled crayfish tails and set aside. Reserve six crayfish heads with claws for decorating the finished dish.

2 In a saucepan, boil sufficient white wine to cover the oysters. Add the oysters and continue boiling until they open. Remove the oyster meat from the shells and set aside.

3 Continue boiling the wine until reduced by half. Add the double cream and continue boiling until reduced by half, then simmer, uncovered, over low heat.

11

4 Heat the oil in a saucepan and sauté the shallots and chanterelles over medium heat for 7 to 8 minutes. Add the cognac and reduce almost all the liquid. Stir in the thyme and the garlic clove. Add the lemon juice and remove the garlic. Add the reduced cream and bring to the boil for a moment. Add the crayfish and oysters to the sauce and stir. Season with salt and pepper to taste.

5 Arrange the shellfish ragoût attractively in the centre of six large, warm plates. Decorate each portion with a reserved crayfish head.

●Ragoûts (from the French *ragoûter*, 'to revive the taste') were traditionally served between courses to stimulate the appetite. A dry Chardonnay may be served.

——— •• ———

VIENNESE SNAIL SALAD

FOR SIX PEOPLE

48 snails, without their shells, rinsed and drained
3 tablespoons wine vinegar
6 tablespoons salad oil, preferably corn or sunflower
salt and freshly ground black pepper to taste
6 eggs, hard-boiled, peeled and chopped

1 tablespoon freshly grated horseradish
1 onion, peeled and finely diced
6 fresh green lettuce leaves, cut into a chiffonade (thin, straight strips, equal in size)

1 Reserve six whole snails for garnishing, and then cut the other snails into thin slices.

2 Prepare a marinade by mixing the wine vinegar, salad oil, and salt and pepper to taste.

3 Place the whole and sliced snails in the marinade for 10 minutes.

4 Remove the six whole snails from the marinade and set aside.

5 Carefully add the chopped egg, horseradish, and onion to

the snail marinade. Gently fold all of the ingredients together.

6 Arrange the lettuce attractively on six chilled plates. Place
the prepared snail salad on the lettuce and pour some marinade
over each serving. Garnish each portion with one whole snail.

●When we think of snails, the standard garlic butter
speciality preparation comes first to mind. Although
known as French speciality, snails have long been
appreciated in Austrian cuisine. We find this snail salad
a welcome and satisfying change.

——— •• ———

MUSSELS WITH PAPAYA IN A POMMERY MUSTARD DRESSING

FOR SIX PEOPLE

18 large New Zealand mussels
  or 42 mussels
4 tablespoons oil for sautéing
4 shallots, peeled and cut into
  thin strips
225 ml (scant ½ pt) dry white
  wine
1 bay leaf
5 black peppercorns
3 ripe papayas

POMMERY MUSTARD DRESSING
2 egg yolks
1 tablespoon tarragon vinegar
300 ml (½ pt) olive oil
3 tablespoons salad oil,
  preferably corn or sunflower
4–5 tablespoons Pommery
  mustard
8 tablespoons soured cream
salt and freshly ground white
  pepper to taste

1 Rinse the mussels under cold running water and debeard
them.

2 Heat the oil in a large saucepan over high flame. Lower the
flame, add the shallots, and sauté until they are transparent.

3 Add the mussels and sauté them quickly, stirring, until the
shells open.

4 Add the wine, bay leaf, peppercorns, and enough water to

cover the mussels completely. Bring to a boil, lower the flame, cover the pan, and allow to simmer for about 7 minutes.

5 Remove the mussels from the pan and cool them in iced water. Pull the mussels from their shells and set aside.

6 Meanwhile, bring the liquid back to a boil and reduce to a quarter of the original amount, producing a thick stock. Strain off the bay leaf and peppercorns. Allow the stock to cool, and set aside.

7 Prepare the dressing: whisk the egg yolks and vinegar in a salad bowl. Add the olive oil drop by drop, whisking all the time. Then stir in the salad oil. Next fold in the mustard and soured cream. Finally dilute the dressing by stirring in 4 tablespoons of the cool reserved mussel stock. Season with salt and pepper to taste.

8 Place the mussels in the dressing and marinate for 10 minutes.

9 Meanwhile, halve and peel the papayas and cut into thin slices. Arrange the papaya slices in attractive fan shapes on six chilled plates. Remove the mussels from the dressing and put two New Zealand or seven mussels on each plate. Coat the mussels and tips of the papaya slices with the Pommery mustard dressing.

●This combination of seafood, cooling papaya slices, and a mustard dressing is also a good main dish for a light lunch or supper. We use the enormous, intense, and succulent New Zealand mussels. If you cannot find the New Zealand variety, use ordinary mussels.

A dry white wine may accompany this dish. Our recommendation is Grüner Veltiner by Bruendelmayer-Malat, or Napa Valley Chardonnay by Robert Mondavi.

———••·———

CALF'S HEAD IN ASPIC WITH A RED ONION VINAIGRETTE

FOR SIXTEEN PEOPLE

½ calf's head (ask your butcher to cut the head lengthways)
1 onion, studded with 2 bay leaves and 10 whole cloves
20 black peppercorns
1 medium carrot, peeled and cut into small cubes
1 medium turnip, peeled and cut into small cubes
2 gherkins, diced
3 egg whites, at room temperature
2 sheets gelatine or 2 envelopes gelatine, dissolved in 8 tablespoons cold water
2 tablespoons wine vinegar

salt and freshly ground white pepper to taste
lettuce leaves

RED ONION VINAIGRETTE
1 medium red onion, peeled and cut into very small cubes
1 teaspoon Dijon mustard
4 tablespoons wine vinegar
170 ml (scant ⅓ pt) olive oil
1 small bunch each of parsley, chives, and chervil, washed, dried, and finely chopped
salt and freshly ground white pepper to taste

1 Remove any remaining hair from the calf's head. Blanch the head by placing it in boiling salted water for 2 minutes. Remove and rinse in cold water.

2 Place the blanched calf's head in a large saucepan, cover with water, and bring to the boil.

3 Add the studded onion and peppercorns. Boil for 15 minutes. Add the carrot and turnip and continue boiling until the meat and vegetables are tender, about 35 minutes. The meat should come off the bone easily.

4 Remove the meat and vegetables from the pan. Discard the onion and peppercorns. Reserve the stock.

5 Pull the meat from the bone and then chop into 1.25 cm (½″) cubes. Mix the meat, carrot, and turnip cubes in a bowl. Add the cubed gherkins. Place this mixture in a 2 litre (3¼ pt) terrine and allow to cool.

6 Boil the reserved stock down until about 300 ml (generous ½ pt) remains; the reduced stock should be thick. Remove from the heat.

15

7 Whisk the egg whites until they are stiff and stir them into the warm, thickened stock. Slowly bring to the boil over medium heat.

8 Stir the dissolved gelatine into the boiling mixture and remove from the heat. Season with the wine vinegar and salt and white pepper to taste.

9 Generously cover the meat and vegetables in the terrine with the gelatine mixture. Cool to room temperature, then refrigerate at least 3 hours.

10 Prepare the vinaigrette: mix the onion, mustard, and vinegar in a bowl. Add the oil, drop by drop, whisking all the while. Stir in the parsley, chives and chervil. Season with salt and pepper to taste.

11 Place two thin slices of the aspic on lettuce leaves on each plate. Drizzle with a tablespoon of the vinaigrette.

●In Austria, calf's head in aspic, known as 'Sulz' is traditional fare often served in *Heuriger*, the wine gardens where good cheer is celebrated in pastoral surroundings. Friends will drive to the wine-growing suburbs of Vienna, Grinzing or Nussdorf, to gather for walks and sit around wooden tables beneath the trees, relaxing and enjoying hearty fare and wine. This Sulz, with a piquant red onion vinaigrette is a flavourful accompaniment for an afternoon bout of drinking. It is a striking addition to a cold buffet and makes great picnic food. Serve with plenty of cold lager or with refreshing spritzers made with chilled white wine and soda.

———·•·———

Tagliolini and Tagliatelle

Pasta and seafood combinations have become increasingly popular. Here are a few of the more interesting and elegant variations. All can double as first courses or main-dish suppers. The perfect wine to serve with these pasta courses is Cabernet Merlot by R. Schlumberger.

——— •·• ———

BASIC RECIPE FOR TAGLIOLINI AND TAGLIATELLE

FOR TWELVE PEOPLE

350 g (12 oz) fine semolina
300 g (10 oz) plain flour
1 teaspoon salt
5 eggs
1 tablespoon olive oil

1 Sift together the semolina, flour and the salt. Place the flour mixture in a mound on a clean surface. Make a well in the centre and put the eggs and oil in the well. Work the liquid ingredients into the flour with your hands. Knead the dough until thoroughly blended. The dough should be firm.

2 Allow the dough to rest for 1 hour and then put through a pasta machine.

●Tagliatelle are 1.25 cm ($\frac{1}{2}$″) wide and 30 cm (12″) long. Tagliolini are of the same width as spaghetti and 37.5 cm (15″) long.

——— •·• ———

17

TAGLIATELLE WITH SMOKED SALMON AND GREEN PEAS

FOR SIX PEOPLE

450 g (1 lb) tagliatelle, bought or home-made (see Index)
350 g (12 oz) fresh young green peas, in their pods
2 tablespoons olive oil
170 g (6 oz) smoked salmon, cut into 1.25 cm (½") cubes

2 tablespoons vodka
8 tablespoons double cream
salt and freshly ground white pepper to taste
juice of ½ lemon (about)

1 Boil the pasta in plenty of salted water until done 'al dente', tender but firm. Strain and refresh in iced water to halt the cooking. Set aside.

2 Meanwhile, shell the peas, then boil 1 minute in salted water, drain, and refresh in iced water.

3 Heat the olive oil in a large saucepan and sauté the salmon over medium heat for 3 to 4 minutes. Add the vodka and reduce for 2 to 3 minutes. Then add the cream and bring to a simmer.

4 Add the peas and season with salt, pepper, and lemon juice to taste.

5 While the sauce is still simmering, add the tagliatelle. Stir the pasta in the sauce a few times to coat it.

6 Serve immediately in warm soup plates.

———— ••• ————

TAGLIOLINI WITH LOBSTER, PRAWNS, AND CRAYFISH

FOR SIX PEOPLE

1 live lobster, weighing 700 g
(1½ lb)
4 live crayfish
3 large prawns
450 g (1 lb) tagliolini, bought or
home-made (see Index)
3 tablespoons butter
2 shallots, peeled and finely
diced

3 tablespoons cognac or brandy
225 ml (scant ½ pt) double cream
juice of 1 lemon
(approximately)
salt and freshly ground white
pepper to taste

1 Place the live lobster head-down in a large saucepan of boiling, salted water. Cook for 5 minutes. Remove and refresh in iced water.

2 Add the crayfish to the boiling water the lobster was cooked in, and boil for 2 to 3 minutes. Remove the crayfish and refresh in iced water.

3 Add the prawns to the boiling lobster water and boil for 2 to 3 minutes. Remove and refresh in iced water.

4 Remove the shells from all the seafood and cut the meat into medium-size cubes. Set aside.

5 Cook the pasta in plenty of boiling, salted water until done 'al dente' tender but firm. Strain and refresh in iced water to halt the cooking. Set aside.

6 Heat the butter in a large frying pan and sauté the shellfish for 1 minute.

7 Add the shallots and cognac or brandy. Flambé: cook over low heat for 1 minute, until the cognac or brandy has warmed. Ignite the spirit, being careful to stand back. Let it burn until the flame is exhausted, about 2 minutes. Remove the shellfish and keep warm in a covered plate.

8 Add the cream to the frying pan. Over medium heat, reduce by about half to a sauce consistency. Add lemon juice and salt and pepper to taste.

9 Stir in the seafood. Add the tagliolini and stir carefully into the sauce a few times, coating it well.

10 Serve immediately in warm soup plates.

●If fresh crayfish are not available, this dish is just as delicious with just lobster or prawns.

————— ·•· —————

TAGLIOLINI WITH MUSSELS, CLAMS, AND CARROTS

FOR SIX PEOPLE

450 g (1 lb) tagliolini, bought or home-made (see Index)
5 tablespoons, olive oil
8 shallots, peeled and thinly sliced
4 garlic cloves, peeled, crushed, and cut in half
30 mussels, rinsed and debearded

225 ml (scant ½ pt) dry white wine
30 clams, rinsed and cleaned
1 large carrot, peeled and finely diced
8 tablespoons double cream
juice of 1 lemon (about)
salt and freshly ground white pepper to taste

1 Cook the pasta in plenty of boiling, salted water until done 'al dente' tender but firm. Strain and refresh in iced water to halt the cooking. Set aside.

2 Heat 2 tablespoons of the olive oil in a saucepan. Add half the sliced shallots and half the crushed garlic cloves. Sauté over medium-high heat for 5 minutes.

3 Add the mussels and sauté until they open.

4 Add the wine and enough water to cover the mussels. Boil for 5 minutes.

5 Remove the mussels and add the clams to the boiling stock. When the clams have opened, remove them and reserve the stock.

6 Take the mussel and clam meat out of the shells and set aside, Keep six nice mussel shells and six nice clam shells for a decoration.

7 Heat the remaining 3 tablespoons olive oil in a large saucepan. Add the remaining shallots and garlic. Sauté briefly.

8 Add the diced carrot and 8 tablespoons of the reserved stock. Reduce by half.

9 Add the double cream and reduce by about half to a sauce consistency. Season with lemon juice and salt and pepper to taste.

10 Stir in the mussels and clams. Add the pasta and carefully stir it in the sauce a few times to coat it.

11 Serve immediately in six warm soup plates. Decorate each portion with a mussel shell and a clam shell.

— •• —

SEAFOOD TERRINE WITH LOBSTER

FOR EIGHTEEN PEOPLE

450 g (1 lb) scallops
450 g (1 lb) lemon sole fillets
4 tablespoons double cream
1 egg white
juice of 1 lemon
1 tablespoon tarragon vinegar

salt and freshly ground white pepper to taste
butter for the terrine
2 lobster tails, weighing a total of 450 g (1 lb)

1 Place the scallops and lemon sole fillets in a food processor. Add the cream, egg white, lemon juice, and vinegar. Purée until the mixture forms a smooth mousse.

2 Press the mousse through a fine sieve, discarding whatever does not pass through. Add salt and white pepper to taste.

3 Preheat the oven to 130 °C/250°F/gas $\frac{1}{2}$.

4 Pour half of the purée into a buttered 2 litre (3 pt) earthenware terrine or $32.5 \times 22.5 \times 5$ cm ($13 \times 9 \times 2''$) loaf tin. Layer the

21

meat of the two lobster tails over this and cover with the remaining purée.

5 Place the terrine in a roasting tin filled with hot water and bake for 30–40 minutes. Remove from the oven and allow to cool.

6 Place a large serving dish at least the same size as the terrine on top and turn upside down to unmould. Before serving, cut the seafood mould into slices about 2 cm ($\frac{3}{4}$″) wide.

——— •∙• ———

COLD SEAFOOD TERRINE WITH RED AND GREEN PEPPER SAUCE

FOR EIGHTEEN PEOPLE

1 kg (2 lbs) filleted turbot
juice of 3 lemons
1 litre (generous 1½ pts) double cream
4 egg whites
2 teaspoons cognac
2 teaspoons dry vermouth
6 tablespoons finely chopped watercress
salt and freshly ground white pepper to taste
1 kg (2 lbs) filleted Dover sole
1 teaspoon saffron, soaked in a teaspoon of dry vermouth for a minimum of 5 minutes, to bring out the colour
1 kg (2 lbs) filleted salmon
butter for the terrine

RED AND GREEN PEPPER SAUCES
6 red peppers, seeded, cored, and finely sliced
6 green peppers, seeded, cored, and finely sliced
2 tablespoons butter
2 tablespoons dry white wine
2 teaspoons dry vermouth
2 teaspoons cognac
675 ml (1¼ pts) double cream
225 ml (scant ½ pt) soured cream
2 teaspoons sherry vinegar
1 teaspoon grated nutmeg
salt and freshly ground white pepper to taste

1 Place the turbot in a food processor with the juice of 1 lemon, a third of the cream, 2 egg whites, 1 teaspoon of the cognac, 1 teaspoon of the vermouth, all of the watercress, and salt and white pepper to taste. Purée until smooth and pass through a fine sieve. Set aside in a bowl.

22

2 Place the Dover sole in the processor with the juice of 1 lemon, a third of the cream, and the remaining 2 egg whites, 1 teaspoon of cognac, and 1 teaspoon of vermouth. Drain the saffron and add it with salt and white pepper to taste. Purée until smooth, strain through a fine sieve, and set aside in a bowl.

3 Place the salmon in the processor with the juice of 1 lemon, the remaining cream, and salt and white pepper to taste. Purée until smooth, pass through a fine sieve, and set aside in a bowl.

4 Preheat the oven to the lowest possible setting.

5 Butter a 2 litre (3 pt) earthenware terrine and line the bottom and sides with greaseproof paper. Layer the pink, green, and yellow seafood mousse for a colourful effect. Cover the top of the terrine with greaseproof paper.

6 Place the terrine in a roasting tin of hot water. Place the tin in the oven and cook for 35 minutes. Remove the terrine from the oven and allow to cool. Unmould by placing a plate of at least the same size as the terrine on top and turn upside down. Peel off the greaseproof paper.

7 To prepare the sauces: in separate pans, over medium heat, sauté the red and green peppers in a tablespoon of butter each for 10 minutes.

8 Add 1 teaspoon each of the wine, vermouth, and cognac to each pan. Add half of the cream of each pan and reduce by half.

9 Separately blend the contents of each pan in a food processor. Strain each through a fine sieve. Set the red and green sauces aside in separate bowls to cool.

10 Stir into each bowl half of the soured cream and then 1 teaspoon of the sherry vinegar. To each bowl add $\frac{1}{2}$ teaspoon of grated nutmeg and salt and white pepper to taste, and stir.

11 Place 2 tablespoons of each sauce on each plate. Shake the plates to swirl the sauces together for a colourful effect. Serve 2 slices of the seafood terrine over the sauce.

———•••———

VEAL AND VEGETABLE TERRINE WITH WATERCRESS SAUCE

FOR TWELVE PEOPLE

450 g (1 lb) lean minced veal
225 ml (scant ¼ pt) double cream
2 egg whites
2 tablespoons Madeira
2 tablespoons cognac
salt and freshly ground white
 pepper to taste
12 runner beans, with both ends
 snapped off
½ medium carrot, peeled and cut
 into 1.25 cm (½″) strips
½ medium turnip, peeled and
 cut into 1.25 cm (½″) strips
½ head cauliflower, cut into
 small florets
2 celery stalks, with any tough
 strings removed from the

sides, cut into 1.25 cm (½″)
 strips the same length as the
 carrot strips
slices of streaky bacon for
 lining the terrine

WATERCRESS SAUCE
5 bunches watercress
8 tablespoons double cream
225 ml (scant ½ pt) soured cream
 or 8 tablespoons soured
 cream plus 4 tablespoons
 crème fraîche
juice of ½ lemon
salt and freshly ground white
 pepper to taste

1 Place the veal, cream, egg whites, Madeira, and cognac in a food processor and purée to a smooth mousse.

2 Pass the mousse through a fine sieve. Add salt and white pepper to taste. Refrigerate.

3 Blanch the beans, carrot, turnip, cauliflower, and celery separately by placing briefly in boiling water and then immediately refresh in iced water. Each vegetable must be blanched and refreshed separately. Keep the vegetables in separate bowls to drain.

4 Preheat the oven to 225°F/110°C/gas ¼.

5 Line a 2 litre (3¼ pt) earthenware terrine with thin slices of streaky bacon, pressing tightly. Pour one quarter of the veal mousse into the terrine. Arrange strips of each vegetable for a colourful effect. Alternate layers of meat and vegetables, ending with meat. Make sure that the sides and ends of the terrine are covered with meat mousse in order to secure the mould.

6 Cover the terrine, place it in a pan of hot water, and bake for 35 to 40 minutes.

7 Allow the terrine to cool. Place a plate at least the same size as the terrine on top and turn upside down to unmould. Rap the plate with the inverted terrine sharply on a work surface once to loosen the mould.

8 Rinse and drain the watercress. Reserve 6–10 sprigs for decoration. Place in a food processor and add the double cream. Blend to the consistency of a thick sauce. Pass through a fine sieve.

9 Stir in the soured cream. Add the lemon juice and stir. Season with salt and white pepper to taste.

10 First pour some sauce on a plate. Cut a slice of the terrine to reveal the beautiful colours, and place on the green sauce. Decorate with a sprig of watercress.

Chapter 2

SOUPS

AUSTRIANS attach great importance to soups, considered the essential beginning of a meal. It is unthinkable to serve a dinner without a good soup, fragrant and fortifying, slowly simmered and prepared with love. The typical every-day Viennese soup is beef bouillon, intensified as a golden consommé, and varied with delicious soup garnishes and dumplings. Bouillon is also the basis for many wonderful thick and creamy soups in the Viennese repertoire. Here are our suggestions for soups to entice the appetite as a separate course or satisfy as a meal in themselves.

——··——

BOUILLON
Klare Rindsuppe

MAKES 2 LITRES (3½ PTS)

1 kg (2 lb) beef bones
2 medium onions, unpeeled
700 g (1½ lbs) beef, rinsed under cold water
½ leek, well washed and trimmed
¼ celeriac, peeled

2 medium carrots, peeled
1 clove garlic, peeled
stems of 1 bunch parsley, rinsed
10 black peppercorns
1 bay leaf
salt to taste

1 Rinse the beef bones under cold water, chop into 7.5 cm (3″) pieces, blanch them in boiling water for 2 minutes, then again rinse in cold water.

2 Cut the unpeeled onions in half. Place the cut sides down over a low flame or cutsides up under a hot grill and allow to char.

3 Place the blanched bones and the beef in a large saucepan

26

with 5 litres (generous 1 gal) cold water. Bring to the boil, lower the heat, and simmer, uncovered, for 2 hours, skimming frequently. Remove the meat.

4 Add the charred onions, leek, celeriac, carrots, garlic, parsley stems, peppercorns, bay leaf, and salt to taste. Cover and continue simmering for another 2 hours.

5 Strain the bouillon first through a sieve and then through cheesecloth.

6 Refrigerate overnight and skim again for the clearest possible consommé.

●This is our basic soup, used all year round in Austria to make consommé and other soups. It is especially fine to come home to on a very cold day. In Austria we serve Klare Rindsuppe decorated with freshly chopped chives or filled with soup garnishes.

——— ·•· ———

CONSOMMÉ
Wiener Kraftsuppe

MAKES 2 LITRES (3¼ PTS)

450 g (1 lb) lean minced beef
1 medium carrot, peeled and finely diced
¼ celeriac, peeled and finely diced
½ bunch parsley, finely chopped
3 egg whites
6 black peppercorns
2 litres (3¼ pts) cold bouillon
Salt to taste

1 Mix the meat, vegetables, egg whites, and enough water so that the mixture is still thick but holds together. Refrigerate for 3 hours.

2 Place this mixture in a saucepan with the peppercorns. Add the cold bouillon. Bring to a boil, stirring frequently. When the boiling point has been reached, stop stirring, and allow the fat to rise to the surface. Simmer the soup for 1½ hours, skimming occasionally.

3 Strain through cheesecloth, discard the solids, season with salt, and bring quickly to a boil.

4 Serve in individual bowls with any of the following traditional garnishes.

●This recipe may be followed to further intensify and clarify the bouillon. In Vienna, consommé is considered the perfect soup for convalescence, being both nourishing and digestible. In restaurants the consommé is served alone or with delicious garnishes such as Fritatten, Leberknödel, or Griessnockerln (recipes follow).

———··———

Traditional Austrian Garnishes for Consommé

FRITATTEN
Pancake Strips

MAKES ENOUGH PANCAKES FOR 12 SERVINGS OF CONSOMMÉ

70 g (2½ oz) flour
425 ml (¾ pt) milk
2 eggs
¼ bunch parsley, finely chopped

salt and freshly ground white pepper to taste
pinch of grated nutmeg
30 g (1 oz) butter for frying

1 Mix the flour, milk, and eggs to a smooth consistency. Stir in the parsley and season with salt, pepper, and nutmeg to taste.

2 Heat a little of the butter in an omelette pan over medium heat and pour in a very thin layer of batter, sufficient to cover the bottom of the pan. Brown on both sides and cut into thin strips while still warm. Repeat with the remaining batter.

3 Float the Fritatten strips on top of the consommé and serve immediately.

———— ·•· ————

LEBERKNÖDEL
Liver Dumplings

MAKES 8–10 DUMPLINGS, 1 PER SERVING OF CONSOMMÉ

3 bread rolls, approximately 60 g (2 oz) each, crusts removed
8 tablespoons milk
225 g (8 oz) calf's liver, with skin and sinews removed
115 g (4 oz) chopped bacon
1 medium onion, thinly sliced
1 tablespoon salad oil
2 eggs

1 clove garlic, peeled and finely chopped
$\frac{1}{2}$ bunch parsley, finely chopped
$\frac{1}{4}$ teaspoon dried marjoram
salt and freshly ground white pepper to taste
70 g (2$\frac{1}{2}$ oz) breadcrumbs
1 litre (generous 1$\frac{1}{2}$ pts) bouillon

1 Crumble the insides of the bread rolls, soak them in the milk, then squeeze out.

2 Mince the liver, bacon, and soaked rolls together. (You can use a food processor.)

3 In a frying pan, fry the onion in the oil over medium-high heat until translucent, about 10 minutes.

4 In a large bowl, mix the minced liver mixture with the eggs, onion, garlic, and parsley.

5 Season with the marjoram and salt and pepper to taste. Thicken with the breadcrumbs and form balls of equal size.

6 In a saucepan, bring the bouillon to a boil, add the dumplings, reduce the heat, and simmer for 10 minutes.

7 Remove the dumplings and serve floating on the Consommé

———— ·•· ————

GRIESSNOCKERLN
Small Semolina Dumplings

MAKES 6–8 DUMPLINGS, 1 PER SERVING OF CONSOMMÉ

1 egg
60 g (2 oz) butter, melted
8 tablespoons coarse semolina

salt to taste
680 ml (1¼ pts) bouillon

1 Beat the egg and butter until frothy. Stir in the semolina and season with salt. Cover and allow to rest 15 minutes.

2 In a saucepan, bring the bouillon to a boil. Form oval dumplings with a spoon and slide them into the bouillon. Reduce the heat and allow to simmer 10 minutes. Remove and quickly refresh in cold water.

3 Serve floating in the consommé.

——— • • • ———

GOULASH SOUP

SERVES 6

2 tablespoons oil for sautéing
3 medium onions, peeled and diced
2 tablespoons tomato purée
4 tablespoons flour
1 tablespoon sweet Hungarian paprika
1 tablespoon red wine vinegar
1.5 litres (scant 2½ pts) bouillon

170g (6 oz) lean beef, cut into 2.5 cm (1″) cubes
1 garlic clove, peeled and crushed
½ teaspoon caraway seeds
½ teaspoon dried marjoram
salt to taste
3 medium potatoes, peeled and cut into 1.25 cm (½″) cubes

1 Heat the oil in a frying pan and sauté the onions until they are golden brown. Add the tomato purée and remove from the heat.

2 Stir in the flour and then the paprika. Add the vinegar and then the bouillon. Stir well and return to the heat.

3 Bring to a boil and add the meat, garlic, caraway, marjoram, and salt to taste. Allow to boil, uncovered, until the meat is tender.

4 Add the potatoes and continue boiling, uncovered, until they are tender but firm.

5 The goulash should be served while piping hot!

●Traditionally thought of as a Hungarian dish, goulash is very much a part of Austrian cuisine. Serve this winter stew as a meal in itself, with crusty rolls and good beer.

—— ·•· ——

POTATO-LEEK SOUP

FOR SIX PEOPLE

2 tablespoons oil for sautéing
1 medium onion, finely sliced
1 leek (white portion only), finely sliced
2 tablespoons flour
1.13 litres (2 pts) Bouillon (see Index)
450 g (1 lb) potatoes, peeled and finely sliced (new potatoes are ideal, but use any red-skinned potato)

8 tablespoons double cream
2 tablespoons butter
$\frac{1}{8}$ teaspoon grated nutmeg
salt and freshly ground white pepper to taste
$\frac{1}{2}$ bunch parsley, finely chopped
croûtons (sauté a finely cubed roll or slice of white bread in butter until golden)

1 Heat the oil in a large saucepan and sauté the onion and leek over medium heat.

2 Stir in the flour and then add the bouillon. Bring to a boil, add the potatoes, and cook until tender, about 25 minutes.

3 Purée the soup in a blender. Return the soup to the saucepan. Add the cream and butter. Heat through over a low flame. Season with the nutmeg and salt and pepper to taste.

4 Serve in individual soup bowls, each portion sprinkled with chopped parsley. Serve the croûtons separately.

● This potato-leek soup served either hot or chilled is a favourite in Austrian households. A subtle hint of nutmeg is necessary, giving this creamy soup its distinctive flavour. The nutmeg should be barely noticeable and never overpowering.

———··———

SOURED CREAM SOUP
Stoss-Suppe

FOR SIX PEOPLE

1.13 litres (2 pts) bouillon
1 teaspoon caraway seeds
425 ml (¾ pt) soured cream
2 tablespoons flour
1 teaspoon red wine vinegar
60 g (2 oz) butter, diced

salt and freshly ground white pepper to taste
croûtons (sauté a finely cubed roll or slice of white bread in butter until golden)

1 In a saucepan, bring the bouillon and caraway seeds to a boil. Blend the soured cream and flour and add to the pan. Stir in smoothly.

2 Simmer, uncovered, over low heat until a soup consistency is reached; this will take about 25 minutes.

3 Stir in the vinegar and season with salt and pepper to taste. Swirl in the butter.

4 Serve in individual bowls, topping with the croûtons.

● One of the most memorable experiences a traveller can have is an autumn train ride from Vienna to Graz, capital of Styria, south-west of Vienna. The train winds through densely forested mountains, glorious with the season's colours—a spectacular panorama. Stoss-Suppe originates in this mountainous region. Our Soured Cream Soup is a version of this Styrian speciality. Vinegar and caraway seeds add a distinctive depth.

CREAM SOUP WITH HERBS AND SWEETBREAD CUBES

FOR SIX PEOPLE

30 g (1 oz) butter
½ onion, thinly sliced
1 leek (white portion only), rinsed very thoroughly and sliced
1½ tablespoons fresh basil leaves, rinsed, patted dry, and finely chopped
½ tablespoon fresh lemon balm leaves, rinsed, patted dry, and finely chopped
½ tablespoon fresh tarragon leaves, rinsed, patted dry, and finely chopped
½ tablespoon fresh sorrel, rinsed, patted dry, and finely chopped

4 tablespoons flour
2 tablespoons red wine vinegar
1 litre (generous 1½ pts) double cream
1 litre (generous 1½ pts) bouillon
1 tablespoon lemon juice
salt and freshly ground white pepper to taste
60 g (2 oz) sweetbreads, cleaned, blanched in boiling water, refreshed in iced water, and cut into 1.25 cm (½″) cubes (4 tablespoons cubed)
½ bunch parsley, finely chopped

1 Heat the butter in a frying pan and sauté the onion and leek over medium heat.

2 Stir in the herbs (except the parsley) and flour and heat through for a minute. Cool with the red wine vinegar.

3 Add the cream and bring to a boil.

4 Add the bouillon, bring to a boil, and reduce to a soup consistency.

5 Season with lemon juice and salt and pepper to taste.

6 Serve in warm soup bowls, over the sweetbread cubes, and garnished with the parsley.

——— •••• ———

33

ASPARAGUS CREAM SOUP

FOR SIX PEOPLE

700 g (1½ lbs) green asparagus, trimmed
¼ teaspoon salt
1.5 litres (scant 2½ pints) chicken stock
85 g (3 oz) butter
4 tablespoons flour

salt and freshly ground white pepper to taste
⅛ teaspoon ground nutmeg
350 ml (generous ½ pt) double cream
2 egg yolks
½ bunch parsley, finely chopped

1 Boil the asparagus in 425 ml (¾ pt) water with ¼ teaspoon salt added, until tender. Lift the asparagus out of the saucepan and drain. Reserve the cooking water. Cut the tips off the asparagus and reserve for garnishing. Cut the asparagus stems into small pieces.

2 Purée the asparagus pieces in a blender or food processor and press through a sieve.

3 In a large saucepan, mix the puréed asparagus with the salted cooking water. Add the chicken stock. bring to the boil and allow to reduce for 15 minutes.

4 Prepare a white roux by melting the butter in a saucepan and stirring in the flour.

5 Ladle 4 tablespoons of the hot stock into the roux and blend thoroughly. Pour this mixture back into the soup, whisking thoroughly. Bring to the boil and reduce to a smooth consistency.

6 Remove the soup from the heat. Season with salt, pepper, and nutmeg to taste. Whisk in the cream and egg yolks.

7 Return to the heat and bring quickly to the boil.

8 Serve in warm soup bowls, garnished with chopped parsley and the asparagus tips.

——— ••• ———

CHAPTER 3

Salads and Salad Dressings

AN IMAGINATIVELY prepared salad, utilising the freshest seasonal produce, refreshes and invigorates the palate. It is a pleasurable experience to search a country garden or city market for the choicest salad ingredients and then to dress them with a balanced vinaigrette.

Our basic vinaigrette is one part vinegar or lemon juice to two parts salad oil. A teaspoon of mustard, crushed garlic, or a fragrant mixture of fresh herbs may of course be added. The following are popular salad dressings, frequently used in Viennese cuisine. Note that the Viennese vinaigrette includes sugar, which intensifies the flavour of tomatoes in a remarkable way.

——— •• ———

VIENNESE VINAIGRETTE

1 part white wine vinegar mixed with an equal amount of water

1 teaspoon caster sugar per 425 ml (¾ pt) of vinaigrette

salt and freshly ground black pepper to taste

2 parts salad oil

Blend well and serve.

——— •• ———

LEMON DRESSING

1 part fresh lemon juice
salt and freshly ground white
   pepper to taste

pinch of sugar
2 parts salad oil

————— • • • —————

EGG DRESSING FOR
VEGETABLE SALADS

MAKES ABOUT 400 ML (SCANT $\frac{3}{4}$ PT)

8 tablespoons vinegar
1 teaspoon Dijon mustard
salt and freshly ground black
   pepper to taste

2 sieved hard-boiled egg yolks
225 ml (scant $\frac{1}{2}$ pt) oil

Blend well and serve. It is especially fine with crudités.

————— • • • —————

SOURED CREAM DRESSING

MAKES ABOUT 300 ML ($\frac{1}{2}$ PT)

2 tablespoons lemon juice
salt and freshly ground white
   pepper to taste

1 tablespoon chopped fresh dill
225 ml (scant $\frac{1}{2}$ pt) soured cream

Blend well and serve. Dill, with its anise overtone, adds great flavour to mixed salads.

————— • • • —————

YOGURT DRESSING

MAKES ABOUT 300 ML ($\frac{1}{2}$ PT)

2 tablespoons lemon juice
salt and freshly ground white
  pepper to taste

1 tablespoon chopped fresh dill
225 ml (scant $\frac{1}{2}$ pt) yogurt

Blend well and serve as a lively dressing for mixed salads.

——— •·• ———

VIENNESE TOMATO SALAD

FOR SIX PEOPLE

12 medium, ripe tomatoes
225 ml (scant $\frac{1}{2}$ pt) Viennese
  vinaigrette

1 large onion, sliced
$\frac{1}{2}$ bunch chives, chopped

1 Dip the tomatoes in boiling water for 5 seconds, refresh in ice water, then peel. Cut into slices or wedges.

2 Pour the vinaigrette into a salad bowl. Mix in the sliced onion and half of the chives.

3 Add the tomato slices and fold carefully.

4 Arrange attractively on individual salad plates and sprinkle with the remaining chives.

●The tomatoes for this salad must be ripe but firm. The warm ruby glow of vine-ripened tomatoes pairs beautifully with a sprinkling of dark green chives fresh from your herb garden. This standard Viennese recipe is appropriate for all meat and poultry dishes.

——— •·• ———

VIENNESE CUCUMBER SALAD

FOR SIX PEOPLE

2 medium cucumbers, peeled
   and thinly sliced
½ teaspoon salt
3 cloves garlic, peeled and
   crushed

3 tablespoons red wine vinegar
½ teaspoon sweet Hungarian
   paprika, or to taste
6 tablespoons olive oil

1 Place the cucumber slices in a salad bowl and sprinkle with salt. Add the garlic, cover the bowl, and allow to rest about ½ hour.

2 Add the vinegar, 1 tablespoon cold water, and paprika to taste. Stir well, add the oil, and stir again.

3 Since this salad has a liquid consistency, serve it in small salad bowls, garnished with a pinch of paprika.

●Garlic adds depth to this salad, a perfect accompaniment for pork dishes or any fried food.

——— ·•· ———

VIENNESE POTATO SALAD

FOR SIX PEOPLE

1 kg (2 lb) red-skinned potatoes
225 ml (scant ½ pt) Viennese
   vinaigrette
1 large onion, chopped
1 bunch chives, chopped

salt and freshly ground black
   pepper to taste
6 large lettuce leaves
sweet Hungarian paprika

1 Boil the potatoes but do not overcook—they should still be firm. Allow to cool, then peel and cut into medium slices.

2 Pour the viennese vinaigrette into a salad bowl. Add the chopped onion and most of the chives (reserve 1 tablespoon for garnishing). Stir well. Season with salt and black pepper to taste.

3 Add the potatoes, stir to coat, and allow to rest 15 minutes.

4 Serve the salad on the lettuce leaves on individual plates. Garnish with the remaining chives and a sprinkling of paprika.

●Austrians love potatoes. If they are not served as a side dish, this potato salad would appear on the table. Use paprika and fresh chives as a colourful and delicious garnish for this salad.

——— •••• ———

VIENNESE POTATO SALAD WITH MAYONNAISE

FOR SIX PEOPLE

1 kg (2 lbs) potatoes (preferably red-skinned)
2 tablespoons red wine vinegar
5 tablespoons mayonnaise

2 gherkins, cubed
salt and freshly ground white pepper to taste
1 gherkin, thinly sliced

1 Boil the potatoes only until still firm. Allow them to cool, and then peel and cut into medium slices.

2 Pour the vinegar and 1 tablespoon water into a large bowl. Add the potatoes and stir well. Allow to rest 15 minutes, stirring frequently.

3 Mix the mayonnaise and cubed gherkins in a separate large bowl.

4 Add the potatoes, mix well, and season with salt and white pepper.

5 Arrange on individual salad plates and garnish with the sliced gherkins.

●This is perfect for a picnic; excellent with chicken and cold meats. We suggest using red-skinned potatoes, which are firm when sliced, adapting well to salads.

——— •••• ———

CUCUMBER SALAD WITH NEW POTATOES

FOR SIX PEOPLE

450 g (1 lb) new potatoes
1 medium cucumber
4 tablespoons red wine vinegar
1 teaspoon salt
freshly ground black pepper to
taste

2 cloves garlic, peeled and
crushed
6 tablespoons olive oil
sweet Hungarian paprika

1 Boil the potatoes, taking care not to overcook them—they should still be firm. Drain the potatoes, allow them to cool, and cut them into slices.

2 Peel and thinly slice the cucumber, reserving six medium slices unpeeled for garnishing.

3 Pour half of the vinegar and 1 tablespoon water in a salad bowl. Add the salt, some freshly ground black pepper, and the garlic. Add the cucumber and potatoes, stir well, and marinate for 15 minutes.

4 Add the remaining vinegar and the oil. Mix well.

5 Place the unpeeled cucumber slices on kitchen paper and sprinkle with paprika.

6 Distribute the salad on chilled plates and garnish with the paprika-cucumber slices.

●A refreshing variation on the classic Viennese cucumber salad, this is also good with fried foods and pork.

———— •·• ————

CHAPTER 4

Seafood

VARIED, low in calories, and high in nutrients, seafood is undeniably granted pride of place in contemporary cuisine. Our stellar chef, Andreas Kisler, first developed a love of fish cooking at La Marée, one of the finest seafood restaurants in Paris. Young and innovative, he has developed seafood recipes that are subtle and distinctly sophisticated.

———— ··· ————

LEMON SOLE IN A LEEK CREAM

FOR SIX PEOPLE

125 g (4½ oz) clarified butter
3 leeks (white portion only), rinsed thoroughly; 2 thinly sliced, and 1 thinly sliced into strips and kept separately from the other 2
6 shallots, peeled and finely diced
3 tablespoons fish stock

4 tablespoons dry vermouth
4 tablespoons dry white wine
225 ml (scant ½ pt) double cream
Juice of 1 lemon
salt and freshly ground white pepper to taste
6 lemon sole fillets, each weighing 170 g (6 oz)
flour for the fish

1 Heat 45 g (1½ oz) of the clarified butter in a frying pan over low heat. Add the sliced leeks and allow to sweat.

2 Add the shallots and continue cooking until transparent.

3 Add the fish stock, vermouth, and white wine. Bring to a very slow boil. Overcook the leek to make sure it is quite soft. This should take about 10 minutes. When the leek is soft, allow the mixture to cool and purée in a blender to a smooth consistency.

4 Transfer the mixture to a saucepan. Add the cream and cook over medium heat until reduced to a sauce consistency. Stir in the lemon juice and season with salt and pepper to taste. Set aside.

5 Dip one side of each lemon sole fillet in flour and shake off the excess. Heat 60 g (2 oz) of the clarified butter in a large frying pan over medium-high heat. Fry the fish first on the floured side until golden, then turn and fry on the other side until golden outside but barely cooked inside. Remove and keep the fish warm on a covered plate.

6 Add the remaining clarified butter to the frying pan and sauté the julienned leek over medium heat for 3 to 4 minutes. Add a few tablespoons of water and allow the leek to blanch.

7 Pour the sauce on six warm plates. Arrange the fish over the sauce and garnish with the strips of leek.

●Serve the dish with a simple green salad and boiled new potatoes, drizzled with melted butter and sprinkled with fresh parsley. A well-chilled dry white wine is a fine accompaniment. We recommend Grinzinger Chardonnay.

———— •●• ————

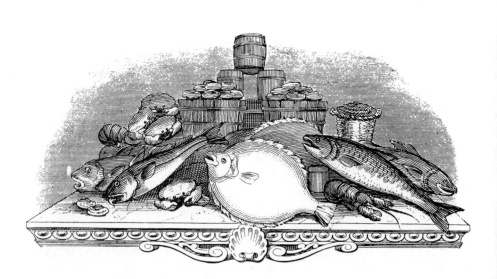

JOHN DORY WITH FENNEL MOUSSE

FOR SIX PEOPLE

115 g (4 oz) clarified butter
2 medium fennel bulbs, thinly
   sliced (reserve the green
   parts for garnishing)
225 ml (scant ½ pt) double cream
2 egg yolks, beaten
3 whole John Dory, with skin
   and bones removed, cut into
   12 fillets
flour for the fish

4 shallots, peeled and finely
   diced
2 tablespoons sherry vinegar
3 tablespoons red wine
4 tablespoons fish stock (see
   Index)
85 g (3 oz) butter, diced
juice of 1 lemon
salt and freshly ground white
   pepper to taste

1 Heat 45 g (1½ oz) of the clarified butter in a frying pan and sauté the fennel over medium heat. Cover the fennel with water and cook until soft. Strain off the water. Place the fennel in a food processor, purée, and strain through a fine sieve.

2 Place the purée in a saucepan, add 6 tablespoons of the cream, and reduce by half. Lower the heat. Slowly stir in the egg yolks, making sure that the mixture does not boil. Set aside.

3 Dip one side of each fish fillet in flour and shake off the excess. Heat 45 g (1½ oz) of the clarified butter in a frying pan and sauté the fish over medium-high heat, first on the floured side, and then on the other side, until golden. Remove the fish and keep warm on a covered plate.

4 Heat the remaining clarified butter and sauté the shallots until golden.

5 Preheat the grill.

6 Add the sherry vinegar, red wine, and fish stock, and reduce almost all of the liquid. Add the remaining cream and reduce to a sauce consistency. Gradually swirl in the butter. Stir in the lemon juice and season with salt and pepper to taste.

7 Spread the fennel mousse over the John Dory fillets and place under the preheated grill until browned and hot inside.

8 Place the fish on six warm plates, surround with the sauce, and garnish with the green fennel tops.

●The flavour of John Dory is similar to that of sole, but its meat is wonderfully firm. We give John Dory the regal treatment, crowning it with a rich and golden fennel mousse.

——— ·•· ———

TROUT 'AU BLEU'

FOR SIX PEOPLE

6 fresh trout, each weighing
　350 g (12 oz), with insides
　removed but left whole
85 g (3 oz) butter
oil for frying the parsley
1 bunch curly parsley
3 lemons, cut in wedges, with
　seeds removed

COURT-BOUILLON
1 litre (generous 1½ pts) fish
　stock
225 ml (scant ½ pt) dry white
　wine

8 tablespoons white vinegar
1 medium carrot, peeled and
　sliced
1 medium celery stalk, sliced
1 medium onion, sliced
1 leek (white portion only), well
　rinsed and sliced
1 teaspoon dill seeds
1 teaspoon fennel seeds
1 bay leaf
1 teaspoon white peppercorns
½ tablespoon salt

1 Place all of the ingredients for the court-bouillon in a saucepan and bring to a boil. Lower the flame, add the trout, and simmer briefly until the trout turn blue and the eyes shrink to button size.

2 Carefully remove the trout from the stock. Dry on kitchen paper and place on six warm plates.

3 Heat the butter in a frying pan over medium heat until it is light brown but not burned.

4 While the butter is browning, heat some oil in another frying pan and fry the parsley over high heat until it is crisp but still green, about 2 to 3 minutes.

5 Pour the browned butter over the trout and decorate with the fried parsley and lemon wedges.

●Austrians especially prize the swiftly moving trout caught fresh from clear mountain streams and quickly poached to achieve the characteristic blue colour (note that a trout that has been frozen will not turn blue when poached). We find that dill and fennel seed give a distinctive perfume to the classic court-bouillon used for poaching. Our trout is drenched with brown butter and decorated with crispy fried parsley and bright wedges of lemon. A leafy salad is all that is needed to complete this simple feast for the nature lover. Uncork a well-chilled Riesling Spätlese.

———— •.• ————

SALMON WITH GLAZED GRAPES

FOR SIX PEOPLE

5 tablespoons grape-seed oil, or,
  if not available, use 75 g
  (2½ oz) clarified butter
6 fillets of salmon, each
  weighing about 200 g (7 oz)
4 shallots, peeled and finely
  diced
60 g (2 oz) seedless black grapes
60 g (2 oz) seedless white grapes
2 tablespoons red wine vinegar

4 tablespoons port
4 tablespoons fish stock
8 tablespoons double cream
juice of 1 lemon
salt and freshly ground white
  pepper to taste
4 tablespoons butter
knob of clarified butter
1 tablespoon sugar

1 Heat 3 tablespoons of the grape-seed oil in a frying pan and sauté the salmon over medium-high heat for 2 to 3 minutes on each side. The fish should remain slightly pink inside. Remove the fish and keep warm on a covered plate.

2 Heat the remaining grape-seed oil in the same frying pan and sauté the shallots until golden.

3 Add half of the black and half of the white grapes. Sauté over medium heat for not more than 2 minutes.

4 Add the vinegar and reduce almost all of the liquid.

5 Add the port and reduce by half.

6 Add stock (with no further reducing). Blend all of the above in a food processor or blender and strain through a fine sieve to remove all the grape skin.

7 Place the mixture in a pan, add the cream, and reduce to a sauce consistency over medium heat. Stir in the lemon juice and season with salt and pepper to taste. Swirl in the 4 tablespoons of butter.

8 Heat the clarified butter in another pan and sauté the remaining grapes over medium heat for not more than 2 minutes. Add the sugar and heat through for a moment.

9 Pour the sauce on six warm plates and arrange the salmon over the sauce. Garnish the fish with the glazed grapes. Serve with rice and salad.

——— ••• ———

PIKE QUENELLES IN DILL SAUCE

FOR SIX PEOPLE

450 g (1 lb) pike fillets
425 ml ($\frac{3}{4}$ pt) double cream
2 egg whites
juice of 1 lemon
1 litre (generous 1$\frac{1}{2}$ pts) fish stock (see index)
225 ml (scant $\frac{1}{2}$ pt) dry white wine
45 g (1$\frac{1}{2}$ oz) clarified butter
6 shallots, peeled and finely diced

$\frac{1}{2}$ bunch fresh dill, chopped without stems (reserve a little finely chopped dill for garnish)
4 tablespoons white vinegar
85 g (3 oz) butter, diced
4 tablespoons whipped cream
pinch of grated nutmeg
salt and freshly ground white pepper to taste

1 Place the pike, half of the cream, the egg whites, and lemon juice in a food processor and purée until smooth. Pass through a fine sieve.

2 Form 18 quenelles by placing 1 tablespoon of fish mixture in the palm of your hand. Smooth it into an oval. Scoop up the fish mixture with a tablespoon and gently place it on a plate. Repeat to form all the quenelles.

3 Place the fish stock and white wine in a large saucepan. Heat to a simmer, add all the quenelles, and poach until tender, approximately 5 minutes. Remove the quenelles and keep warm on a covered plate. Reserve the poaching liquid.

4 Heat the clarified butter in a frying pan and sauté the shallots over medium heat until golden. Add the dill and sauté for 1 minute. Pour in the poaching liquid (there should be about 680 ml ($1\frac{1}{4}$ pts)) and reduce by half. Add the remaining cream and reduce to a sauce consistency. Add the vinegar. Gradually swirl in the butter and then strain the sauce into another pan.

5 Carefully fold in the whipped cream and finish the sauce with grated nutmeg and salt and pepper to taste.

6 Place the quenelles on six warm plates and spoon sauce over them. Garnish with the chopped dill.

●The meat of the pike is sweet and firm, ideally suited for forming these fluffy dumplings. The fish is so low in calories that it makes up for the cream that we use in the smooth binding of dill, an aromatic emphasis for the fish. Serve with a julienne of seasonal vegetables. A dry white wine is the suitable accompaniment.

If pike is not available, we suggest using lemon sole or, less expensively, flounder.

———·•·———

RED SNAPPER IN CITRUS SAUCE WITH JULIENNE OF VEGETABLES

FOR SIX PEOPLE

225 ml (scant ½ pt) dry white wine
225 ml (scant ½ pt) dry vermouth
1 bay leaf
6 white peppercorns
1 medium carrot, cut into thin strips
1 fennel bulb, cut into thin strips
1 celeriac cut into thin strips
juice of 2 lemons
juice of 2 limes

juice of 1 orange
225 ml (scant ½ pt) double cream
2 chicory, cut into thin strips
30 gl (1 oz) butter, diced
2 tablespoons Dijon mustard
salt and freshly ground white pepper to taste
3 tablespoons clarified butter
6 fillets of red snapper or bream, each weighing 180 g (6 oz)
flour for the fish

1 Pour 680 ml (1¼ pts) of water and the white wine and vermouth into a medium-sized saucepan, and add the bay leaf and peppercorns. Bring to a boil and then strain off the bay leaf and peppercorns. Return to a boil and cook the carrot, fennel, and celeriac separately until tender. When each vegetable is done, remove from the stock, refresh in iced water, and set aside separately. Reserve the stock.

2 Raise the flame under the stock. Add all of the citrus juices and the cream. Reduce to a sauce consistency. Add the blanched vegetables. Bring to the boil and immediately remove from the flame.

3 Add the chicory. Swirl in the butter and then swirl in the mustard. Season with salt and pepper to taste. Set aside and keep warm on the stove top. To prevent the mustard from forming lumps, do not allow the sauce to cook.

4 Heat the clarified butter in a frying pan. Dip the meat side of each fish fillet in the flour. Briefly fry the fish on the skinless side for 2 to 3 minutes and then turn and fry on the skin side until crisp and tender.

5 Place the fish on six warm plates and cover with the vegetable sauce.

LANGOUSTINES IN A PERNOD-GINGER SAUCE

FOR SIX PEOPLE

2 tablespoons unsweetened bottled or fresh lime juice

1 tablespoon very finely diced fresh root ginger

1 leek (white portion only), finely diced

1 medium, carrot, peeled and finely diced

1 medium turnip, peeled and finely diced.

18 langoustines or Dublin Bay Prawns, not larger than 85 g (3 oz) each, or 18 large prawns

4 tablespoons dry white wine

4 tablespoons Pernod

225 ml (scant ½ pt) double cream

3 tablespoons clarified butter for frying

salt and freshly ground white pepper to taste

3 limes, cut in wedges, for garnishing

1 Combine the lime juice and the ginger cubes. Set aside.

2 Bring 1 litre (generous 1½ pts) of water to a boil in a medium saucepan. Add the cubed vegetables and the langoustines. Cook for 2 minutes over low heat. Remove the langoustines and refresh in iced water. Remove the tails from the body and take out the tail meat. Set aside. Twist off the claws and reserve for a garnish. Reserve 4 tablespoons of the stock.

3 Remove the vegetables from the stock and set aside. Reserve 4 tablespoons of the stock.

4 Pour the reserved stock into a saucepan. Add the white wine and Pernod. Reduce by half. Add the ginger and half of the lime juice it was soaking in. Add the cream and reduce to a sauce consistency. Swirl in the vegetables.

5 Heat the clarified butter in a frying pan. Sauté the langoustine meat for 2 to 3 minutes over high heat. Season with salt and pepper to taste.

6 Place langoustine meat in the centre of each warm plate with a set of claws above and below it, pincers facing in opposite directions. Place lime sections between the pincers. Cover the meat with the ginger sauce.

●These langoustines should be served alone, elegantly garnished with claws and lime sections. The sauce is also delicious with lobster if you can't find langoustines.

———— •·• ————

SOFT-SHELL CRABS WITH ALMOND SAUCE

FOR SIX PEOPLE

12 soft-shell crabs
flour for dipping
salt and freshly ground white
  pepper to taste
60 g (2 oz) butter
toasted almond slivers for
  garnish

ALMOND SAUCE
small knob of butter
70 g (2½ oz) almonds, blanched
  and finely ground

2 tablespoons Amaretto liqueur
4 tablespoons white wine
4 tablespoons fish stock or
  bottled clam juice
juice of 1 lemon
juice of ½ grapefruit
4 tablespoons plain yogurt
8 tablespoons soured cream
salt and freshly ground white
  pepper to taste

1 Rinse the crabs and pat dry with kitchen paper. Season the flour with salt and pepper. Roll each crab in the flour, shake off the excess, and set aside.

2 Begin the almond sauce: melt the butter in a saucepan over low heat. Add the ground almonds and sauté for 5 minutes. Add the Amaretto, wine, fish stock, and lemon and grapefruit juices and stir well. Bring to a boil over high heat and continue boiling for 2 to 3 minutes to allow the alcohol to evaporate. Set aside to cool.

3 Melt the butter in a large frying pan over medium heat. Add the crabs to the frying and sauté for 2 to 3 minutes on each side, until golden brown. If the crabs are small, you can sauté them all at once; otherwise, do six at a time. Remove the crabs to a covered dish and keep warm.

4 Finish the almond sauce: mix the yogurt and soured cream in a large bowl. When the almond sauce has reached room

temperature, slowly stir it into the yogurt mixture. Season with salt and pepper to taste.

5 Spoon some sauce on each plate and top with two crabs. Sprinkle with toasted almonds.

●Soft-shell crabs are a speciality of the American east coast, especially the Chesapeake Bay area. They are not a separate species, but crabs which are caught shortly after 'moulting' or shedding their too-small shells in order to grow a new one. If you are lucky enough to come across them, this is a delicious way to treat them. It can also be adapted for shelled crabs.

————··——

BASS STUFFED WITH FENNEL, WITH A CLAM SAUCE

FOR SIX PEOPLE

6 thick fillets of bass, each weighing 225 g (8 oz)
1 kg (2 lb) clams, cleaned
250 ml (scant ½ pt) dry white wine
6 teaspoons beef marrow
115 g (4 oz) clarified butter for frying
1 head fennel, thinly sliced (reserve the leaves from the fennel head for decoration)
pinch of fennel seeds
6 tablespoons dry vermouth
8 tablespoons brown veal stock

6 slices white bread, with crusts removed, cut into 1.25 cm (½″) cubes
3 egg yolks
2 shallots, peeled and thinly sliced
1 clove garlic, peeled and crushed
225 ml (scant ½ pt) double cream
3 tablespoons cognac
flour for the fish
juice of 1 lemon
salt and freshly ground white pepper to taste

1 Lay the bass fillets on a flat surface and make an incision lengthways on the top of each fillet, holding your knife at an angle. This will make a flap under which you can place the stuffing.

2 Boil the clams in 680 ml (1¼ pts) of water and 225 ml (all but 2 tablespoons) white wine until the shells open. Refresh in iced water and remove the clam meat from the shells. Reserve the meat and discard the shells.

3 Blanch the marrow briefly in boiling water, refresh in iced water, and dice.

4 Heat 45 g (1½ oz) of the clarified butter in a frying pan over medium-high heat and sauté the fennel slices and fennel seeds for 8 to 10 minutes. The fennel should be soft but not browned. Add the vermouth and veal stock. Allow to reduce over medium heat for 10 minutes.

5 With your hands, mix the bread cubes and marrow into a mass. Add this to the fennel. Stir to mix.

6 Remove the frying pan from the heat. Slowly whisk in the egg yolks. Set aside to cool.

7 Heat 30 g (1 oz) of the clarified butter in a frying pan and sauté the shallots and garlic over medium heat for 4 to 5 minutes. Add the clam meat and the remaining white wine. Stir in the cream and bring to a very slow boil. While it is boiling, add the cognac. Continue boiling until a sauce consistency is reached.

8 While the sauce is boiling, place some fennel stuffing in each fish fillet and seal the fillet with a wooden cocktail stick. Dip the fish on the stuffed side in some flour.

9 Heat the remaining clarified butter in a frying pan and fry the fish on the floured side over medium-high heat until golden. Turn and fry on the other side until golden. Remove and keep warm on a covered plate.

10 Pour the sauce into the frying pan, in which the fish has been fried. Stir in the lemon juice and season with salt and pepper to taste.

11 Pour the clam sauce onto six warm plates. Place the stuffed fish fillets over the sauce, remove the cocktail sticks, and decorate with the reserved fennel leaves.

●This is a recipe contributed by Peter Moser, master chef at the Palais Schwarzenberg, one of Vienna's most elegant restaurants. In the midst of the busy capital, this baroque palace and its garden are a magic setting for culinary adventure. Serve this impressive stuffed fish with a simple dish of buttered new potatoes.

● Mussels could be used if clams are not available.

———— •• ————

MEDALLIONS OF LOBSTER IN A DILL-CUCUMBER SAUCE WITH CHICKEN MOUSSE QUENELLES

FOR SIX PEOPLE

2 lobsters each weighing 1.3 kg (2½ lb)
8 boneless and skinless chicken breasts
3 eggs
300 ml (½ pt) double cream
juice of 1 lemon
salt and freshly ground white pepper to taste
2 medium cucumbers, peeled, with seeds removed, and diced
4 tablespoons dry white wine
½ bunch fresh dill, finely chopped
1 tablespoon sherry vinegar
2 garlic cloves, puréed in a food processor with 5 tablespoons olive oil

1 Cook the lobsters in boiling water for 10 to 12 minutes. Reserve *all* of the resulting stock and separate 8 tablespoons of it for use in the sauce. Remove the tail meat from the lobsters and cut into 5 medallions, about 2.5 cm (1″) thick, per person. Set aside. Remove the meat from the claws and cut in half lengthwise. Set aside separately.

2 Purée the chicken breasts, eggs, 8 tablespoons of the double cream, and the lemon juice in a food processor until smooth. Pass through a fine sieve into a bowl. Season with salt and pepper to taste. Place the bowl in a larger bowl filled with ice and chill for 1 hour.

3 Place 1 teaspoon of the chicken mixture in the palm of your hand. Smooth it into an oval. Scoop up the mixture with another teaspoon and gently place it on a plate. Repeat to form all the quenelles.

53

4 Reheat the reserved lobster stock (less the 8 tablespoons for the sauce) to a simmer and gently add the quenelles. Poach in the simmering stock until tender, about 5 minutes. Remove the quenelles carefully with a slotted spoon and set aside on a covered plate.

5 Blanch the cucumber cubes briefly in boiling salted water. Strain and then liquefy in a blender. Set aside.

6 Pour the remaining double cream, the white wine, and the reserved lobster stock into a pan. Cook over a medium flame until reduced by half, about 8 to 10 minutes. Add the liquefied cucumber and continue reducing to a sauce consistency, about 8 to 10 minutes. Finish the sauce with the chopped dill and sherry vinegar. Season with salt and pepper to taste.

7 While the sauce is reducing, heat the garlic oil in a frying pan and briefly reheat the lobster medallions. Set aside on a covered plate. Briefly reheat the claw meat and set aside separately.

8 Pour the cucumber sauce onto six warm plates. Place the five lobster medallions for each serving over the sauce and top them with claw meat. Arrange three quenelles on each plate.

SALMON STEAK IN PUFF PASTRY WITH A SORREL SAUCE

FOR SIX PEOPLE

450 g (1 lb) puff pastry
  (readymade is acceptable)
1.13 kg (2½ lb) fresh salmon, cut
  into 6 steaks, with skin and
  bones removed, and
  sprinkled with salt and
  pepper
2 egg yolks, beaten with 2
  tablespoons water
100 g (3½ oz) clarified butter
4 shallots, peeled and finely
  sliced

1 bunch fresh sorrel, sliced in
  3 cm (1¼″)-thick strips
4 tablespoons red wine vinegar
4 tablespoons dry white wine
8 tablespoons fish stock (see
  Index)
8 tablespoons double cream
juice of 1 lemon
salt and freshly ground white
  pepper to taste

1 Preheat the oven to 200°C/400°F/gas 6.

2 Roll the puff pastry into 12 squares; six squares should be the size of the fish steaks and the other six should be slightly larger on each side, to overlap.

3 Place the salmon on the small squares of pastry. Brush the sides of the squares with the beaten egg yolks. Cover with the larger pastry squares and then press to seal. Brush the top of the pastry with the egg yolks.

4 Heat 70 g (2½ oz) of the clarified butter in a large ovenproof frying pan or gratin dish. Place the salmon in pastry in the frying pan and fry over medium heat for 5 minutes on the bottom side only. Transfer to the preheated oven and bake for 8 to 10 minutes. Remove the pastry packets and keep warm on a covered plate.

5 Meanwhile heat the remaining clarified butter in a saucepan. Sauté the shallots over medium heat until golden. Add half of the sorrel strips and sauté briefly. Add the red wine vinegar, white wine, and fish stock. Cook over medium heat for 5 minutes, or until reduced by half. Add the cream and continue cooking 5 to 7 minutes, until reduced to a sauce consistency.

6 Strain the sauce into a second pan. Stir in the lemon juice and season with salt and pepper to taste.

7 Pour the sorrel sauce onto six warm plates and place the salmon in pastry over the sauce. Arrange the remaining, uncooked sorrel around the pastry.

●Serve with boiled new potatoes and an array of seasonal vegetables. This is a dish that merits a festive Champagne.

———··———

SALMON FILLETS WITH A PRAWN RAGOÛT

FOR SIX PEOPLE

1 kg (2 lb) fresh salmon, with skin and bones removed, cut into 18 equal fillets
white breadcrumbs for breading
3 tablespoons olive oil for frying
18 medium-sized fresh prawns, peeled and deveined, cut into 2.5 cm (1″) pieces
4 garlic cloves, peeled and puréed in a processor with 2 tablespoons olive oil

4 shallots, finely chopped
4 tablespoons dry white wine
4 tablespoons fish stock
4 tablespoons double cream
6 medium cup mushroom caps, cut in half
juice of 1 lemon
salt and freshly ground white pepper
½ bunch parsley, finely chopped

1 Dip the salmon fillets in the white breadcrumbs and shake off any excess. Heat the olive oil in a frying pan and sauté the fillets over medium-high heat for 2 to 3 minutes until they are golden outside and pink inside. Remove the fillets and keep warm on a covered plate.

2 Sauté the prawns in the garlic oil. Add the shallots and sauté until golden. Remove the prawns and shallots and set aside.

3 Add the white wine and the stock to the frying pan. Reduce by half. Add the cream and reduce to a sauce consistency. Add the mushrooms and allow to simmer for 1 minute. Stir in the lemon juice, prawns, and shallots. Season with salt and pepper to taste.

4 Pour the ragoût sauce on six warm plates and place the fillets over the ragoût. Garnish with the chopped parsley

Chapter 5

Veal and Calves' Liver

Pearlescent, tender, and free of fat, veal is healthy yet delicate fare, more digestible than beef or pork, and simple to prepare. The subtle flavour of this meat makes it ideally suited for combination with a limitless variety of sauces and seasonings. Viennese cuisine is particularly renowned for its Schnitzel preparations, veal cutlets as delicious as they are quick and easy to prepare. Here we offer several beloved Austrian standard recipes, as well as our own newer variations.

——— ••• ———

NATURSCHNITZEL

FOR SIX PEOPLE

12 escalopes, each weighing 100 g (3½ oz), from the fillet end of leg of veal
flour
clarified butter for frying
4 tablespoons dry white wine for degreasing

3 tablespoons brown veal stock (see Index)
60 g (2 oz) butter, diced
salt and freshly ground white pepper to taste

1 Pound the cutlets and make two incisions in the edge of each to prevent shrinkage.

2 Dip one side of each in some flour and shake off the excess. Heat a knob of clarified butter in a frying pan and sauté several escalopes on the floured side until golden outside but still pink inside, about 2 to 3 minutes. Turn and fry 2 to 3 minutes more on the other side. Add clarified butter as needed for frying the rest of the escalopes. Remove and keep warm on a covered plate.

3 Degrease the frying pan by adding the white wine. Add the consommé and reduce by half. Add the veal stock and again reduce by half, swirl in the butter. Season with salt and pepper to taste. Pour any veal juices from the covered plate into the sauce and heat through.

4 Place two escalopes on one side of each individual plate and cover with sauce.

● A flawless delight for the purist. The simple sauce of clear broth and veal stock emphasises the natural delicacy of the cutlets. We recommend the Naturshnitzel with the rice of your choice, such as pressed white rice or Mushroom Rice. A good wine to drink with many veal dishes is a light Austrian Pinot Blanc.

——— ·•· ———

PAPRIKASCHNITZEL

FOR SIX PEOPLE

12 escalopes, each weighing 100 g (3½ oz), from the fillet end of leg of veal
2 tablespoons finely diced smoked bacon
2 medium onions, finely diced
2 tablespoons sweet Hungarian paprika
dash of white vinegar

6 tablespoons consommé
8 tablespoons double cream
juice of 1 lemon
salt and freshly ground white pepper to taste
clarified butter for frying
flour
6 tablespoons dry white wine

1 Pound the escalopes and make two incisions in the edge of each to prevent shrinkage.

2 Sauté the smoked bacon over medium heat, add the onions, and sauté until golden. Add the paprika and sauté 2 to 3 minutes. (If the paprika is allowed to sauté too long, it has a bitter taste.) Add the vinegar and consommé. Reduce almost all of the liquid. Add the cream and reduce to a sauce consistency. Add the lemon juice and salt and pepper to taste.

3 Heat a knob of clarified butter in another frying pan. Dip one side of each in some flour and shake off the excess. Fry the escalopes on the floured side over medium-high heat until golden, about 2 to 3 minutes. Turn and fry on the other side until golden. Remove and keep warm on a covered plate.

4 Degrease the pan by wiping out with kitchen paper. Add the white wine and reduce almost all of the liquid. Strain the prepared sauce into the frying pan. Add the escalopes and their juice. Heat through.

5 Serve the escalopes on six warm plates, covered with the sauce.

●Serve this mildly spicy classic dish with Spaetzle or buttered noodles.

————•••————

KAISERSCHNITZEL

FOR SIX PEOPLE

zest of 3 lemons (make sure not to include any of the white portion of the peel), cut into thin strips
1 teaspoon sugar
1 kg (2 lb) loin or fillet end of leg of veal, cut into 12 escalopes
clarified butter for sautéing
1 small onion, finely sliced

8 tablespoons dry white wine
2 tablespoons capers and their liquid
225 ml (scant ½ pt) double cream
2 tablespoons brown veal stock
juice of 1 lemon
salt and freshly ground white pepper to taste
½ bunch parsley, finely chopped

1 Place the lemon zest in a saucepan. Cover with water and the sugar. Boil until the zest has a slightly sweet taste. Remove the zest from the water and allow to cool.

2 Pound the veal and make two incisions in the edge of each escalope to prevent shrinkage.

3 Heat a knob of clarified butter in a frying pan and sauté the veal escalopes over medium-high heat until brown outside and pink inside, about 1½ minutes for each side. Remove and keep warm on a covered plte.

4 Degrease the pan by wiping out with a paper towel. Heat 30 g (1 oz) clarified butter and sauté onion over medium-high heat until golden. Add the white wine and reduce by half. Strain the capers and set aside. Add the caper liquid and reduce 2 to 3 minutes. Reduce the heat to medium, add the cream, and reduce by half, about 8 to 10 minutes.

5 Strain the sauce into second frying pan. Add the veal stock and allow to reduce 1 minute over medium heat. Stir in the lemon juice and lemon zest, and season with salt and pepper to taste.

6 Arrange the escalopes on six warm plates and cover with the sauce. Garnish each cutlet with some parsley and capers.

●Garnished with capers and parsley, this is a pretty dish and can be served with Spaetzle or buttered noodles. The Kaiserschnitzel is enhanced by a medium-dry white wine.

——·•·——

WIENER SCHNITZEL

FOR SIX PEOPLE

6 escalopes, each weighing 170 g (6 oz), from the loin of veal
2 eggs
2 tablespoons milk
flour and breadcrumbs for coating

salt and freshly ground white pepper to taste
170 g (6 oz) butter
170 ml (scant ⅓ pt) oil
3 lemons for garnish

1 Pound the veal escalopes with a steak beater. Make two incisions in the edge of each cutlet to prevent shrinkage during the frying.

2 Beat the eggs and milk in one bowl. Place the flour and breadcrumbs separately in two more bowls.

3 Season the meat. First dip the escalope in the bowl of flour and shake off the excess. Next dip the escalope in the egg-milk mixture. Again shake off the excess. Finally dip the escalope in breadcrumbs and shake off the excess. The crumbs should cling only slightly to the escalope.

4 Heat half of the butter and half of the oil in a frying pan over a high heat until quite hot, 165°C (325°F). Fry three escalopes about 3 minutes on each side, until golden brown, and then drain on paper towels. Pour out the fat and wipe out the pan with paper towels. Add the remaining butter and oil. Heat over a high heat until hot. Sauté the remaining escalopes as you did the first. Drain them on paper towels.

5 Serve garnished with lemon wedges.

●Breaded veal escalopes, fried to golden perfection. This simple and rewarding dish was imported into Austria from Milan in the early nineteenth century. It quickly became the national favourite, the *ne plus ultra* of Viennese cuisine. Decorate the cutlets with bright lemon wedges and serve the traditional way with a leaf or cucumber salad.

SLICED VEAL STEAKS IN MOREL SAUCE WITH POTATO DUMPLINGS

FOR SIX PEOPLE

450 g (1 lb) potatoes
150 g (5 oz) flour (approximately)
1 egg yolk
salt and freshly ground white pepper to taste
3 tablespoons sherry vinegar
8 tablespoons double cream
1 bunch basil, finely chopped
75 g (2½ oz) clarified butter for sautéing
700 g (1½ lbs) loin of veal, sliced into 6 steaks

6 shallots, peeled and finely diced
85 g (3 oz) fresh morels, sliced into fine strips, or 15 g (½ oz) dried morels, soaked in Madeira at least 30 minutes, and then sliced into fine strips
4 tablespoons Madeira
225 ml (scant ½ pt) brown veal stock
30 g (1 oz) butter, diced

1 Boil the potatoes until tender and then peel them. Allow the potatoes to cool. Pass through a meat mincer or a ricer and set aside.

2 Mix the minced or riced potatoes, 70 g (2½ oz) of the flour, and the egg yolk to form the dough. Knead the dough on the work surface, adding flour as necessary, up to 150 g (5 oz), until the dough no longer sticks to the surface. Salt and pepper to taste.

3 Form the dough into 30 small round dumplings. Drop the dumplings into boiling salted water, return to the boil, and cook for 4 or 5 minutes. Remove and refresh in iced water.

4 Pour the sherry vinegar into a saucepan, add the cream, and bring to a boil over medium-high heat. Reduce to a sauce consistency. Add the potato dumplings, chopped basil, and salt and pepper to taste. Keep warm over a low flame.

5 Heat 3 tablespoons clarified butter in a frying pan and sauté the veal steaks over high heat until they are brown outside and pink outside, about 7 to 10 minutes. Remove and keep warm on a covered plate.

6 Degrease the frying pan by wiping it out with kitchen paper and add the remaining clarified butter. Sauté the shallots over medium heat until golden. Add the morels and sauté 3 to 4 minutes. Add the Madeira and reduce almost all of the liquid. Add the veal stock, bring to a boil, and cook 3 to 4 minutes, until reduced by half. Swirl in the 30 g (1 oz) butter. Salt and pepper to taste.

7 Carve the veal steaks in half lengthways. Leave one side whole and carve the other into four slices still attached at the bottom, forming a fan shape. Place the dumplings and their sauce on the plate near the veal. Pour some meat sauce on the other side of the plate.

●Two sauces distinguish this dish. An aromatic basil-cream enhances the potato dumplings, and a heady reduction of forest mushrooms, Madeira, and stock accompanies the veal. Serve with an attractive array of seasonal vegetables. We find that a full-bodied white wine is a good accompaniment. Try a Gewürztraminer.

———— ••• ————

MEDALLIONS OF VEAL WITH CHIVES AND CREAM SAUCE

FOR SIX PEOPLE

115 g (4 oz) clarified butter
115 g (4 oz) smoked ham, finely
   diced
6 medium shallots, finely diced
60 g (2 oz) finely diced
   cultivated cup or button
   mushroom caps
8 tablespoons dry white wine
1 bay leaf

8 tablespoons double cream
juice of 1 lemon
6 tablespoons brown veal stock
1.13 kg (2½ lbs) boned saddle of
   veal, cut into 18 medallions
45 g (1½ oz) butter
2 bunches of chives, chopped
salt and freshly ground white
   pepper to taste

1 Heat 60 g (2 oz) clarified butter and sauté the smoked ham. Add the shallots and mushrooms and continue to sauté until they are golden.

2 Add 6 tablespoons white wine and the bay leaf. Reduce almost all of the liquid. Add the cream and bring to a boil. Immediately strain the sauce, reserving the ham, onions, and mushrooms. Discard the bay leaf.

3 Reduce the cream to a sauce consistency. Add the lemon juice and the veal stock, and again reduce to a sauce consistency. Add the ham, mushrooms, and shallots. Set aside.

4 Sauté the veal medallions in the remaining clarified butter over medium-high heat until they are brown outside and pink inside, about 3 to 4 minutes on each side.

5 While the medallions are cooking, heat the 45 g ($1\frac{1}{2}$ oz) of butter in a pan, add the chives, and sauté gently 1 minute, being careful that the butter does not burn. Keep warm.

6 When the medallions are done, set aside on a covered plate. Degrease the pan with the remaining white wine. Add the prepared sauce and any meat juices that have run onto the covered plate. Season with salt and pepper to taste.

7 Place three medallions on the centre of each warm plate. Top one with sautéed chives and one with sauce, and leave one plain.

●A classic demanded again and again by our guests. Lots of gently sautéed chives and a light cream sauce with smoked ham and mushrooms complement the choice veal. Serve with seasonal vegetables and Truffle Crêpes.

MEDALLIONS OF VEAL WITH ASPARAGUS SABAYON IN RIESLING SAUCE

FOR SIX PEOPLE

85 g (3 oz) clarified butter for sautéing

1.13 kg (2½ lbs) tenderloin or top round of veal, cut into 18 medallions

4 shallots, peeled and finely diced

8 tablespoons Riesling

225 ml (scant ½ pt) double cream

8 tablespoons brown veal stock

2 tablespoons Madeira

60 g (2 oz) fresh or preserved goose liver

salt and freshly ground white pepper to taste

ASPARAGUS SABAYON

225 g (8 oz) asparagus, trimmed

knob of clarified butter for sautéing

2 shallots, peeled and finely diced

juice of 1 lemon

4 egg yolks

6 tablespoons double cream

salt and freshly ground white pepper to taste

1 Cook the asparagus in double their volume of water until tender. Drain the asparagus and cut into 1.25cm (½") pieces.

2 Heat the clarified butter in a pan and sauté the 2 shallots over medium heat until golden. Add the asparagus and sauté for 5 minutes.

3 Place the asparagus, shallots, lemon juice, and egg yolks in a food processor and purée thoroughly. Transfer to a bowl and whisk the asparagus mixture with the 6 tablespoons double cream. Season with salt and pepper to taste.

4 Heat half of the clarified butter in a frying pan and sauté the medallions over medium-high heat until they are brown outside and pink inside, about 3 minutes on each side, adding more clarified butter as necessary. Keep warm on a covered plate.

5 Preheat the grill.

6 Degrease the frying pan by wiping it out with a kitchen paper. Heat 2 tablespoons clarified butter and sauté the 4 shallots until golden. Add the Riesling and reduce by half. Add

the cream and reduce by half. Add the veal stock and Madeira and again reduce by half.

7 Whisk in the goose liver and immediately remove the sauce from the heat. Season with salt and pepper to taste.

8 Cover twelve of the medallions with the asparagus sabayon and brown under the preheated grill.

9 Strain the sauce onto six warm plates. For each portion, serve two medallions with sabayon and a plain medallion on top of the sauce.

●Delectable sautéed medallions of veal are covered with a smooth asparagus sabayon (which can be made in advance). The whole is sauced by a Riesling cream with an opulent touch of goose liver. A spring dish whch recalls the fine dining of the Belle Epoque. Serve with an attractive julienne of seasonal vegetables, Château Potatoes and a dry Austrian Riesling.

VEAL STEAKS WITH CHANTERELLES IN A BASIL-MINT SAUCE

FOR SIX PEOPLE

115 g (4 oz) clarified butter for sautéing

1.13 kg (2½ lbs) boned saddle of veal, cut into 6 steaks

170 g (6 oz) fresh chanterelles, rinsed, dried on kitchen paper, and torn in half by hand

5 shallots, peeled and finely chopped

pinch of ground thyme

1 clove garlic, peeled

½ bunch parsley, finely chopped

juice of 1 lemon

salt and freshly ground white pepper to taste

1 bunch fresh basil, rinsed, dried, and finely chopped

1 tablespoon fresh peppermint, rinsed, dried, and finely chopped

dash of sherry vinegar

6 tablespoons dry white wine

225 ml (scant ½ pt) double cream

8 tablespoons brown veal stock

60 g (2 oz) butter, diced

1 Heat 60g (2 oz) clarified butter in a frying pan and sauté the veal steaks over medium-high heat until brown outside and pink inside, about 3 to 4 minutes on each side. Remove and keep warm on a covered plate.

2 Degrease the pan by wiping it out with kitchen paper. Heat 45 g (1½ oz) clarified butter and sauté the chanterelles. Add half of the chopped shallots and dash of thyme. Sauté until golden brown. Spear the garlic on a kitchen fork and stir through the mixture for 2 to 3 minutes. Add the parsley, lemon juice, and salt and pepper to taste. Allow to reduce for 2 minutes. Remove the mushrooms and any remaining sauce and keep warm on a covered plate.

3 Degrease the pan again and heat the remaining clarified butter. Sauté the remaining shallots until golden. Add the basil and mint. Sauté 2 to 3 minutes. Add a dash of sherry vinegar and the white wine. Reduce almost all of the liquid. Add the cream and reduce to a sauce consistency. Add the veal stock and again reduce to a sauce consistency. Gradually swirl in the butter and season with salt and pepper to taste. Set aside and keep warm to allow the flavours to meld.

4 Arrange chanterelles in the centre of each warm plate. Place a veal steak over the chanterelles and strain the sauce all around the mushrooms.

●A memorable summer celebration! Seasonal vegetables and Simple Potato Croquettes are suitable side dishes. For a wine we recommend a Grüner Veltliner Spätlese. Or serve a light white wine with a hint of sweetness.

———— ••• ————

VEAL WITH GLAZED SPRING ONIONS

FOR SIX PEOPLE

6 spring onions (both green and white parts), thinly sliced
85 g (3 oz) clarified butter for sautéing
4 tablespoons dry white wine
8 tablespoons double cream
170 g (6 oz) butter

salt and freshly ground white pepper to taste
1 kg (2¼ lb) fillet of veal, cut into 6 medallions
7 spring onions (green portion only), thinly sliced
1 tablespoon sugar

1 Blanch the white portion of the 6 spring onions in boiling salted water for 3 to 5 minutes. Refresh in iced water, drain, and set aside.

2 Preheat the oven to 200°C/400°F/gas 6.

3 Begin by preparing the sauce: heat 30 g (1 oz) clarified butter in a frying pan and sauté the green portion of the spring onions over medium-high heat for 3 to 4 minutes. Add the white wine and allow to boil for 5 minutes. Purée in a food processor, strain, and return to the frying pan, Add the double cream and reduce by half. Swirl in 150 g (5 oz) of the butter. Season with salt and pepper to taste. Set aside and keep warm.

4 Heat 60 g (2 oz) clarified butter in another, overproof frying pan or gratin dish and quickly sauté the veal over medium-high heat on both sides until golden. Place the frying pan or gratin dish in the preheated oven for about 6 minutes. The veal should be browned outside and pink inside. Remove the veal and keep warm on a covered plate.

69

5 To the same frying pan add the remaining 30 g (1 oz) butter and allow to brown slightly, Sauté the blanched and all the remaining spring onions. Add the sugar and heat through a moment, until the spring onions are glazed.

6 Carve the veal diagonally, from the top corner on one side to the bottom corner on the opposite side. You will have roughly 2 triangles for each piece. Pour the spring onion sauce in the centre of six warm plates. Arrange the veal slices in a circular pattern over the sauce. Place the glazed spring onions in the middle of each serving.

●Serve this light summer dish with a bouquet of seasonal vegetables.

————·•·————

SLICED CALVES' LIVER IN WALNUT SAUCE

FOR SIX PEOPLE

4 tablespoons oil for frying
1.13 kg (2½ lb) calf's liver, with skin and sinews removed, and cut into 12 slices
3 tablespoons flour
30 g (1 oz) butter
4 shallots, peeled and sliced
30 g (1 oz) ground walnuts

2 tablespoons sherry vinegar
3 tablespoons Frangelico liqueur
225 ml (scant ½ pt) brown veal stock
salt and freshly ground white pepper to taste
12 walnut halves for garnish

1 Heat 2 tablespoons of the oil in a frying pan. Dip both sides of the liver slices in the flour and shake off the excess. Fry half the liver slices over medium-high heat for 2 minutes on each side, until brown outside and still pink inside. Remove and keep warm on a covered plate. Heat the remaining oil and repeat with the remaining liver slices.

2 Degrease the frying pan by wiping it out with kitchen paper. Melt the butter and sauté the shallots over medium heat until golden. Add the ground walnuts and allow to brown. Add the sherry vinegar and Frangelico, and reduce by half. Add the stock and reduce all of the liquid to 8 tablespoons. Season with salt and pepper to taste.

3 Cut each fried liver slice diagonally in the middle and arrange four half slices in a star shape on each warm plate. Strain the sauce over the liver and garnish with the walnut halves.

●Ground walnuts provide dramatic texture and flavour, while hazelnut liqueur and sherry vinegar add a fine sweet-piquant note to this uncomplicated liver dish. Serve with glazed carrots or spinach. A rosé or light red wine is recommended.

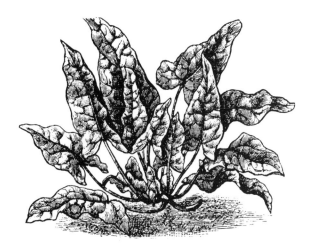

SAUTÉED SWEETBREAD AND CHICKEN MOUSSE DUMPLINGS IN VERMOUTH SAUCE

FOR SIX PEOPLE

1 kg (2 lbs) sweetbreads, cleaned
1 medium carrot, diced
1 stick of celery, diced
1 medium onion, diced
1 leek (white portion only), well rinsed and diced
10 black peppercorns
1 bay leaf
dash of white vinegar
4 boneless and skinless chicken breasts
2 egg whites
350 ml (generous ½ pt) double cream
juice of 1 lemon

2 tablespoons of Madeira
salt and freshly ground white pepper to taste
about 130 g (4½ oz) clarified butter for sautéing
85 g (3 oz) fresh chanterelles, rinsed, dried on paper towels, and torn in half by hand
85 g (3 oz) fresh shiitake mushrooms, sliced
85 g (3 oz) mushrooms, sliced
4 shallots, peeled and finely chopped
pinch of fresh thyme
8 tablespoons dry vermouth

1 Blanch the sweetbreads in 1 litre (generous 1½ pts) boiling water with the diced vegetables, peppercorns, bay leaf, and vinegar. The sweetbreads should be white outside and pink inside. Refresh the sweetbreads in iced water and then cut them in twenty four slices, four per person. Set aside. Reserve all the sweetbread stock resulting from the blanching. Separate 4 tablespoons of the stock and reserve it for the sauce.

2 Cut the chicken breasts into 2.5cm (1″) strips and place with the egg whites, 8 tablespoons of the cream, half the lemon juice, the Madeira, and salt and pepper in a food processor. Purée until smooth. Press the mousse through a fine sieve. Place 1 tablespoon of the mousse in the palm of your hand. Smooth it into an oval. Scoop up the mousse with another tablespoon and gently place on a plate. Repeat to form 18 quenelles. Bring the sweetbread stock (less the 4 tablespoons) to a slow boil and poach the quenelles for 5 minutes, until tender. Refresh the quenelles in iced water, remove, and set aside.

3 Heat 85 g (3 oz) clarified butter in a pan and sauté all of the mushrooms, the shallots, and a pinch of thyme over medium heat for 10 minutes. Add the vermouth and reduce almost all of the liquid. Add the reserved sweetbread stock and allow to reduce for 4 or 5 minutes. Add the remaining cream and reduce to a sauce consistency. Stir in the remaining lemon juice. Season with salt and pepper to taste.

4 Heat 45 g (1½ oz) clarified butter in a frying pan and briefly reheat the sweetbreads. Add the quenelles and sauté 2 to 3 minutes.

5 Pour the sauce onto warm plates and serve three dumplings and four slices of sweetbreads over the sauce.

● An interesting array of mushrooms accompanies our delicate sweetbreads. Serve with seasonal vegetables and Truffle Crêpes (see Index).

CHAPTER 6

Chicken

CHICKEN has many virtues. It is inexpensive, always available, low in calories, easy to prepare, and appropriate at any time of the year. Our recipes demonstrate that, far from being pedestrian, chicken can be the basis for exciting combinations with fruit, herbs, and seasonings. We know you'll enjoy our fried chicken with tarragon sauce, serene chicken with tart apple slices, savoury paprika chicken, mellow thin slices of chicken in Riesling, and zesty chicken with ginger. Each has its own distinctive appeal and may be handsomely presented with the simplest side dishes. The following recipes are fun to prepare and perfect for parties or informal family dinners.

There are several good wines which complement most chicken dishes: Grüner Veltliner, Pinot Blanc, Riesling, Pinot Chardonnay, or Gumpoldskirchner, among them.

CHICKEN BREAST IN TARRAGON SAUCE

FOR SIX PEOPLE

150 g (5 oz) clarified butter for sautéing
12 cup mushrooms, sliced
juice of 1 lemon
60 g (2 oz) butter
4 tablespoons flour, plus flour to coat the chicken
8 tablespoons chicken stock
salt and freshly ground white pepper to taste
6 boneless and skinless chicken breasts, each weighing 225 g (8 oz)
2 eggs
breadcrumbs for coating
4 shallots, peeled and finely chopped
1 bunch tarragon, chopped
2 tablespoons tarragon vinegar
225 ml (scant ½ pt) double cream
5 tablespoons brown veal stock
1 bunch parsley, finely chopped

1 To prepare the velouté, first heat 60 g (2 oz) clarified butter in a frying pan and briefly sauté the mushrooms over medium heat for 3 to 4 minutes. Add the lemon juice and remove the pan from the heat. Set aside.

2 Melt the 60 g (2 oz) of butter in a saucepan. Stir in the flour and then the chicken stock. Allow the stock to boil for 5 minutes. Add the mushrooms and lemon juice. Allow to boil another minute. If the velouté becomes too thick (like double cream) stir in a little water. Season with salt and pepper to taste.

3 While the velouté is still quite hot, spoon it over the chicken breasts. Set aside and allow to cool.

4 Place some flour, the eggs, and some breadcrumbs in separate bowls. Dip the chicken breasts in flour and shake off the excess. Then dip them in the egg and again shake off the excess. Finally dip the breasts in breadcrumbs and shake off the excess.

5 Heat 60 g (2 oz) clarified butter in a frying pan and sauté three of the chicken breasts over medium-high heat until they are golden brown, about 3 to 4 minutes on each side. Remove the breasts and keep warm on a covered dish. Repeat with the remaining breasts.

6 Heat the remaining clarified butter in a saucepan and sauté the shallots over medium heat until golden. Add the tarragon and tarragon vinegar and allow to reduce 4 to 5 minutes. Add the cream and reduce to a sauce consistency. Stir in the parsley and season with salt and pepper to taste.

7 Pour the sauce onto six warm plates and serve the chicken over the sauce.

● Since the early eighteenth century, Backhendl, golden fried chicken garnished with lemon wedges, has been a staple of Viennese cuisine. This is a variation of the Austrian favourite. Boneless chicken breasts are first smoothed with a mushroom velouté, then breadcrumbed and fried the traditional way. Fresh tarragon is essential. Decorate our Backhendl with glazed carrots, broccoli, or Truffle Crêpes.

———•••———

CHICKEN BREAST PRINZ EUGEN

Chicken with Apples in Calvados Cream Sauce

FOR SIX PEOPLE

about 125 g (4½ oz) clarified butter for sautéing
6 chicken breasts, each weighing 225 g (8 oz), boned and skinned
2 eating apples, peeled, cored, and sliced in 5 cm (2″) thick sections (cut the peel into slivers and reserve it for making the sauce)
4 shallots, finely chopped
6 tablespoons Calvados
4 tablespoons chicken stock
225 ml (scant ½ pt) double cream
salt and freshly ground white pepper to taste
30 g (1 oz) butter, diced

1 Preheat the oven to 260°C/500°F/gas 9.

2 Heat 60 g (2 oz) clarified butter in an ovenproof frying pan and sauté 3 of the chicken breasts over medium-high heat, first on the meat side and then on the skin side, about 3 to 4 minutes on each side. Transfer the chicken to the oven and bake for 10 minutes. Heat another 30 g (1 oz) clarified butter and repeat with the remaining 3 breasts. Remove and keep warm on a covered plate.

3 Heat 45 g (1½ oz) clarified butter in the same pan and sauté the apple slices over medium heat. Remove and keep warm on a covered plate.

4 Next sauté the shallots and apple peel until the shallots are golden. Add the Calvados and chicken stock. Reduce by half. Add the cream and reduce to a sauce consistency. Strain the sauce into another pan. Season with salt and pepper to taste. Swirl in the 30 g (1 oz) butter.

5 Cut each chicken breast into five slices. Place an apple slice between each two slices of chicken and cover with the Calvados sauce.

● This dish was named for the Austrian hero of the late seventeenth and early eighteenth centuries Prince Eugène, who was responsible for the building of one of the most beautiful palaces in Vienna, the Belvedere.

Tender slices of white meat alternate with slices of sautéed apple mellowed with a seductive apple-brandy cream sauce. This easy combination of poultry, fruit, and Calvados evokes the bountiful orchards of Normandy. Try it with white rice and a leaf salad. A pleasing wine to accompany this meal is a light, dry Pinot Blanc.

——— •• ———

PAPRIKAHUHN
Paprika Chicken

FOR SIX PEOPLE

8 tablespoons vegetable oil for sautéing

3 whole smallish chickens, cut in half, backbones removed

salt and freshly ground white pepper to taste

4 medium onions, sliced

2 red peppers, with seeds removed, diced

1 tablespoons tomato purée

2 tablespoons sweet Hungarian paprika

550 ml (1 pt) chicken stock or more

225 ml (scant ½ pt) double cream

1 Preheat the oven to 150°C/300°F/gas 2.

2 Heat 60 g (2 oz) oil in a frying pan. Season the chicken with salt and pepper. Sauté on the meat side over medium-high heat for 7 to 8 minutes, until golden; turn, and sauté on the other side for 7 to 8 minutes, until golden. Rmove the chicken from the pan.

3 Degrease the pan by wiping it out with kitchen paper. Sauté the onions in 60 g (2 oz) oil over medium heat until golden. Add the red peppers and sauté 4 to 5 minutes. Stir in the tomato purée. Add the paprika and immediately pour in 350 ml (generous ½ pt) of the chicken stock. Reduce by half. Add the double cream and reduce to a sauce consistency.

4 Arrange the chicken in an ovenproof dish. Pour the remaining chicken stock over it, add the sauce, cover, and bake 30 minutes. Check occasionally to make sure that the sauce is not becoming too thick. Add a little chicken stock or water if necessary.

5 Remove the chicken and set aside on a covered plate. Strain the sauce and blend it to a smooth consistency.

6 Carve the chicken and serve with the paprika sauce and a generous helping of Spaetzle.

● This chicken goulash needs nothing more than Spaetzle to make a simple yet delicious meal. Paprika is a mainstay of Austro-Hungarian cooking. We suggest using sweet Hungarian paprika for authenticity.

———— •·• ————

THIN SLICES OF CHICKEN WITH RIESLING SAUCE

FOR SIX PEOPLE

1 carrot, peeled and cut into thin strips
$\frac{1}{2}$ celeriac, cut into thin strips
$\frac{1}{2}$ turnip, peeled and cut into thin strips
1 parsley root, cut into thin strips
6 chicken breasts, each weighing 225 g (8 oz), boned and skin removed

salt and freshly ground white pepper to taste
85 g (3 oz) clarified butter
1 large onion, thinly sliced
10 white mushroom caps, sliced
225 ml (scant $\frac{1}{2}$ pt) Riesling
225 ml (scant $\frac{1}{2}$ pt) double cream
4 tablespoons chicken stock
15g ($\frac{1}{2}$ oz) butter

1 Separately blanch the strips of vegetables in boiling water, then refresh in iced water. Combine once they are cooled.

2 Cut the chicken breasts against the grain into 1.25 cm ($\frac{1}{2}$")-thick slices. Season with salt and pepper to taste.

3 Heat 60 g (2 oz) clarified butter in a frying pan and sauté the chicken over medium-high heat on each side until golden. Remove and set aside on a covered dish.

4 Add the remaining clarified butter to the frying pan and sauté the onion and mushrooms. Add the Riesling and vegetables. Reduce all of the liquid. Remove the vegetable mixture and set aside.

5 Add the cream and chicken stock to the frying pan. Reduce to a sauce consistency. Blend the sauce, and add the chicken and vegetables. Season with salt and pepper to taste. Reheat a moment, then swirl in the butter.

● Riesling gives brilliant, fruity flavour to this classic one-dish cassoulet of chicken and vegetables. Serve with

Spaetzle and accompany with the same wine used for cooking.

————•••————

CHICKEN CUTLETS ENHANCED WITH GINGER AND SPRING ONIONS

FOR SIX PEOPLE

225 ml (scant ½ pt) unsweetened bottled lime juice
juice of 1 fresh lime
1 medium fresh ginger root
6 chicken breasts, each weighing 225 g (8 oz)
12 spring onions
½ medium carrot, peeled and cut into thin round slices
2 medium sticks of celery, strings removed, and finely sliced

1 leek (white portion only), well rinsed and finely sliced
salt and freshly ground white pepper to taste
100 g (3½ oz) clarified butter
6 spring onions (white portion only), finely sliced
425 ml (¾ pt) chicken stock
4 tablespoons double cream
60 g (2 oz) butter, diced

1 Mix the bottled lime juice and the juice of the fresh lime in a bowl. Peel the ginger root and julienne. Marinate in the lime juice for 1 hour.

2 Bone the chicken breasts, cover with plasticised film, and pound very thin.

3 Cut off the white portion of the spring onions and set aside for garnishing. Chop the green portion.

4 Place the chicken in a large pan. Pour the lime juice and ginger over it. Add the chopped green spring onions, carrot, celery, and leek. Cover and marinate in the refrigerator for 12 hours or overnight.

5 Remove the chicken; sprinkle with salt and pepper. Heat 60 g (2 oz) clarified butter in a frying pan and sauté the chicken over medium heat, for about 3 to 4 minutes on each side. Set aside on a covered plate.

6 Heat 45 g (1½ oz) clarified butter and sauté the white portion of the 6 spring onions over medium heat for 4 to 5 minutes. Strain the vegetables from the marinade and sauté for 4 to 5 minutes.

7 Add the remaining marinade to the vegetables and spring onions. Reduce almost all of the liquid. Add the chicken stock and reduce by half. Add the cream and reduce to a sauce consistency. Gradually swirl in the butter to bind the sauce.

8 Arrange the chicken on six plates, pour the sauce over it, and garnish with the reserved spring onions.

● We find that the classic oriental pairing of ginger and spring onions marries beautifully with the delicate cream sauce used in occidental cuisine. Serve with boiled new potatoes. Our wine recommendation: Riesling Spätlese Ried-Klaus by Josef Jamek.

CHAPTER 7

Game Birds and Animals

SINCE the Middle Ages, game dishes have been an essential part of Austrian cuisine. Originally only the land-owning aristocracy, who retained the sole privilege of hunting, could enjoy this fare. During the nineteenth century, however, hunting became open to everyone, and recipes for game dishes could be found in the cookery books of the middle class. In the 1880s the Wildbretmarkt, the game market in Vienna, became famous across the empire for its variety of rabbit, quail, duck, venison, and other game delicacies.

Today hunting remains a popular sport in Austria. Here we have included some traditional recipes as well as recipes we artfully designed to enhance the rich and sublime flavours of game.

The best wines to accompany game are Jochinger St-Laurent, Cabernet-Merlot, Austrian Pinot Noir, Blau-Fränkisch, Corton, Vosne-Romanée, Beaune, Clos des Mouches, Cabernet Sauvignon.

—— • • ——

DUCK BREAST AND BLUEBERRY SAUCE

FOR SIX PEOPLE

6 boned duck breasts
salt and freshly ground white
  pepper to taste
2 tablespoons oil for sautéing
1 teaspoon sugar
1 teaspoon sherry vinegar
2 teaspoons cassis

225 ml (scant ½ pt) brown veal
  stock
425 ml (¾ pt) double cream
115 g (4 oz) blueberries, rinsed,
  drained, and patted dry on
  kitchen paper
30 g (1 oz) butter, diced

1 Preheat the oven to 200°C/400°F/gas 6.

2 Make a cross-shaped incision on the skin side of each duck breast and sprinkle with salt and pepper.

3 Heat the oil in an ovenproof frying pan or flameproof gratin dish and sauté the duck breasts over medium-high heat, first on the skin side and then on the side without skin, about 4 to 5 minutes on each side. Place the pan or dish in the preheated oven for 4 to 5 minutes, until the breasts are browned outside and pink inside. Keep the duck warm, skin side down, on a covered plate.

4 Pour off the fat from the frying pan or gratin dish. Add the sugar, sherry vinegar, and then the cassis. Reduce by half. Add the stock and reduce to a third of the original amount. Add the cream and blueberries and reduce to a sauce consistency. Swirl in the butter and season with salt and pepper to taste. Strain the sauce and keep it warm over a low heat.

5 Pour the blueberry sauce onto six warm plates. Cut the duck breast against the grain into thin slices and arrange in fan shapes over the sauce.

●Serve with wild rice, Potato Croquettes Rolled in Almonds, or seasonal vegetables. Our wine recommendation: Pinot Noir Spätlese by Klosterkeller Siegendorf. Or serve a soft, medium-bodied red wine.

————— ••• —————

DUCK BREAST AND PLUM SAUCE

FOR SIX PEOPLE

12 duck breasts, boned (reserve the bones to prepare a stock)
salt and freshly ground white pepper to taste
8 plums, with stones removed
2 tablespoons oil for sautéing

2 tablespoons sugar
2 tablespoons sherry vinegar
4 tablespoons plum brandy
120 ml (scant $\frac{1}{3}$ pt) duck stock
30 g (1 oz) butter, diced

1 Preheat the oven to 200°C/400°F/gas 6.

2 Make a cross-shaped incision on the skin side of each duck breast. Sprinkle with salt and pepper.

3 Cut two plums into small cubes and cut the remaining six in halves for garnishing.

4 Heat the oil in an ovenproof frying pan or flameproof ramekin dish and sauté the duck breasts over medium-high heat, first on the side without the skin and then on the skin side, for 4 to 5 minutes on each side. Place the pan or dish in the preheated oven for 4 to 5 minutes, until the duck is browned outside and pink inside. Keep the duck breasts warm on a covered plate, skin side down to prevent further cooking.

5 In the frying pan or gratin dish, sauté the plum cubes and sugar over medium heat. Add the sherry vinegar and reduce by half. Add the plum brandy and reduce by half. Add the duck stock and reduce to a sauce consistency. Swirl in the butter, season with salt and pepper, and strain the sauce. Pour the sauce into a pan.

6 Add the twelve plum halves to the saucepan and poach over medium heat for a minute. Remove the plums from the sauce and keep warm on a covered plate.

7 Pour the plum sauce onto six warm plates. Cut the duck breast against the grain into thin slices (aiguillettes). Arrange the duck in fan shapes on the sauce and garnish each portion with two plum halves, also cut in fan shapes.

——— •• ———

POUSSINS STUFFED WITH CHICKEN MOUSSE AND CHANTERELLES

FOR SIX PEOPLE

6 tablespoons double cream
1 boneless chicken breast, weighing 225 g (8 oz), with fat removed
1 egg yolk
7 tablespoons oil for sautéing
60 g (2 oz) fresh chanterelles, rinsed, dried on paper towels, and torn in half by hand
2 shallots, peeled and finely diced
pinch of thyme
salt and freshly ground white pepper to taste

6 poussins, each weighing 450 g (1 lb), boned, leaving breast and leg whole (your butcher can do this for you), with bones reserved for preparing stock
4 shallots, cut in slices
1 tablespoon tarragon vinegar
225 ml (scant ½ pt) chicken stock made with the reserved poussin bones, or tinned consommé
115 g (4 oz) butter, diced
1 bunch fresh tarragon, rinsed, dried, and finely chopped

1 Place the double cream and chicken breast in a food processor and purée to a smooth consistency. Press through a fine sieve, then stir in the egg yolk and set aside.

2 Heat 1 tablespoon oil in a frying pan and sauté the chanterelles over medium heat for 4 minutes. Add the diced shallots, and brown. Season with a dash of thyme and salt and white pepper to taste. Set aside to cool.

3 When the chanterelles and shallots are cool, mix with the chicken mousse.

4 Preheat the oven to 190°C/375°F/gas 5.

5 Cut off the bony leg tips of the poussins. Stuff the birds with the mousse and sew them shut so the filling doesn't ooze out.

6 Heat 2 tablespoons oil in a frying pan and sauté three of the birds over medium-high heat for 3 to 4 minutes on each side, until brown. Heat another 2 tablespoons oil and repeat with the remaining birds. Place all the birds in a roasting tin and roast in the oven for 15 minutes. When cooked, remove and keep warm on a covered plate.

7 Meanwhile, heat the remaining oil in a frying pan and sauté the sliced shallots until transparent. Add the tarragon vinegar and reduce almost all of the liquid.

8 Add the stock, bring to a boil, and reduce by half.

9 Gradually swirl in the butter. Stir in the tarragon, and set aside.

10 Cut each poussin in half lengthways. Pour some sauce on each plate. Place one half poussin mousse side up and the other mousse side down over the sauce.

●This memorable dish is delicious served on a crisp autumn evening with Champagne Cabbage, wild rice, seasonal vegetables, or Duchesse Potatoes. A full-bodied red wine enhances the poussins.

QUAILS WITH WALNUT STUFFING IN FRANGELICO SAUCE

FOR SIX PEOPLE

9 tablespoons oil for sautéing
4 tablespoons ground walnuts
2 tablespoons ground hazelnuts
2 tablespoons whole pine nuts
450 g (1 lb) white bread, crust removed and cut into 1.25 cm (½″) cubes
4 tablespoons double cream
2 egg yolks
1 whole egg
salt and freshly ground white pepper to taste

12 quails, boned from the backbone, leaving the breasts whole (your butcher can do this), with bones reserved for preparing stock
6 shallots, peeled and thinly sliced
2 tablespoons Frangelico (hazelnut) liqueur
1 teaspoon sugar
1 teaspoon sherry vinegar
225 ml (scant ½ pt) quail stock or strong chicken stock
small knob of butter

1 Heat 2 tablespoons of oil and sauté all of the nuts over medium heat for 2 to 3 minutes. Set aside and allow to cool.

2 Soak the bread cubes in the double cream until soft. Add the egg yolks and whole egg. Stir the mixture and then mash the bread cubes.

3 Add the bread mixture to the cooled nuts. Season with salt and pepper to taste.

4 Preheat the oven to 200°C/400°F/gas 6.

5 Stuff the quails with the bread and nut mixture. Wrap a piece of aluminium foil over the back of each quail and around both ends to seal in the mousse.

6 Heat 3 tablespoons oil in a frying pan and sauté 6 quails breast side down over medium-high heat until browned, about 4 to 5 minutes. Add a further 2 tablespoons oil and repeat with the remaining quails. Place all the birds, aluminium side down, in a roasting tin and roast in the preheated oven for 5 to 7 minutes. Remove from the oven and keep the quails warm on a covered plate.

7 In a frying pan, heat the remaining oil and sauté the shallots over medium heat until transparent, about 5 minutes. Add the Frangelico and the sugar. Bring to a boil for a moment.

8 Add the sherry vinegar and reduce almost all of the liquid. Add the stock, bring to a boil, and reduce to a sauce consistency.

9 Swirl in the butter. Season with salt and pepper to taste. Strain the sauce through a sieve.

10 Remove the foil from the quails. Pour some sauce on each plate. Serve six quails whole and six cut in half lengthways. Place a whole quail in the centre of each plate with a half on either side.

● Brillat-Savarin once said of these game birds: 'A plump little quail pleases equally for its taste, its form, and its colour.' We find this quail stuffed with a mixture of nuts particularly pleasing. A fitting wine is the light Pinot Noir Spätlese by Klosterkeller-Siegendorf.

———··———

QUAIL AND PIGEON BREASTS WITH GREEN FIGS

FOR SIX PEOPLE

8 fresh green figs, rinsed and peeled
4 tablespoons oil for sautéing
12 boned quail breasts, with bones reserved for preparing the stock
12 boned young pigeon breasts, with bones reserved for preparing the stock

4 tablespoons port
1 tablespoon sugar
1 teaspoon sherry vinegar
225 ml (scant ½ pt) quail or pigeon stock or brown veal stock
30 g (1 oz) butter
salt and freshly ground white pepper to taste

1 Cut six of the peeled figs in half. Scrape off and reserve the seeds for cooking. Leave two peeled figs whole.

2 Heat the oil in a frying pan and sauté the boned quail and pigeon breasts over medium-high heat for about 4 to 5 minutes, until brown outside and pink inside. Keep warm on a covered plate, skin side down.

3 In the frying pan, briefly sauté the six halved figs, about 3 to 4 minutes. Add the port, bring to a boil, and poach over medium heat for 30 seconds.

4 Add the two whole figs to the frying pan, as well as the fig seeds, sugar, and sherry vinegar. Reduce by half. Add the stock and again reduce by half. Strain the sauce, swirl in the butter, and season with salt and pepper to taste.

5 Carve the pigeon and quail breasts against the grain into thin slices. Pour the sauce onto six warm plates and arrange the meat in fan shapes on the sauce. Garnish each portion with two poached fig halves.

●The plump sweetness of fresh figs intensifies the flavour of these little game birds. Serve simply with glazed carrots or mange tout. A full-bodied red wine is all that's needed to round out this autumnal meal.

———·•·———

The following are recipes for autumn assortments of game with fruit or herbs, scented truffles or wild mushrooms. These dishes celebrate the abundance of forest and orchard.

ESCALOPES OF VENISON WITH LENTILS AND CHANTERELLES

FOR SIX PEOPLE

1 small carrot, peeled
½ small turnip, peeled
½ leek (white portion only), well rinsed and trimmed
6 tablespoons oil for sautéing
12 escalopes from the fillet end of leg of venison, each weighing 85 g (3 oz), pounded and sprinkled with salt and pepper
3 shallots, peeled and finely sliced

115 g (4 oz) lean bacon, cut into fine cubes
60 g (2 oz) chanterelles, rinsed, dried on kitchen paper, and torn in half by hand
8 tablespoons dry red wine
225 ml (scant ½ pt) brown game stock
salt and freshly ground white pepper to taste
60 g (2 oz) butter, diced
6 tablespoons boiled lentils

1 Blanch the carrot, turnip, and leek separately in boiling water, then refresh in iced water. Mince and set aside.

2 Heat 3 tablespoons oil in a frying pan and sauté half the venison escalopes over medium-high heat until browned outside and pink inside, about 2 to 3 minutes each side. Remove and keep warm on a covered plate. Add the remaining oil and repeat with the remaining escalopes.

3 Add the shallots, bacon cubes and chanterelles to the frying pan and sauté for a moment. Remove and also keep warm on a separate covered plate.

4 To prepare the sauce, add the red wine to the frying pan and reduce by half over medium heat. Add the stock and again reduce by half. Stir any juices from the venison on the covered plate into the sauce. Season with salt and pepper to taste, then gradually swirl in the butter. Add the blanched vegetables, the boiled lentils, and the mixture of chanterelles, shallots, and bacon. Bring to a boil and cook 2 to 3 minutes.

5 Place two escalopes on each warm plate. Cover one with sauce and leave the other plain.

●Robust in character, this venison may be accompanied by Potato Noodles, Viennese Red Cabbage, Champagne Cabbage, or luxurious Truffle Crêpes.

———··•··———

RABBIT SADDLE FILLETS AND PHEASANT BREASTS IN MARJORAM SAUCE

FOR SIX PEOPLE

125 ml (scant ¼ pt) oil for sautéing

3 boned saddles of rabbit, sprinkled with salt and pepper

6 pheasant breasts, boned, sprinkled with salt and pepper

60 g (2 oz) chopped onion

3 tablespoons chopped fresh marjoram

1 tablespoon sherry vinegar

225 ml (scant ½ pt) brown game stock

4 tablespoons red wine

60 g (2 oz) butter, diced

salt and freshly ground white pepper to taste

1 Preheat the oven to 200°C/400°F/gas 6.

2 Heat 60 g (2 oz) oil in an ovenproof frying pan or flameproof gratin dish and sauté the rabbit fillets over medium-high heat for approximately 3 minutes on each side. The rabbit should remain pink inside. Remove and keep warm on a covered plate.

3 In the same frying pan or dish, add another 45 g (1½ oz) oil and sauté the pheasant breasts over medium-high heat for 3 to 4 minutes on each side. Place the pan or dish in the oven for 4 to 5 minutes. Remove the pheasant and keep warm with the rabbit on the covered plate.

4 To prepare the marjoram sauce, heat the remaining oil in the same frying pan and sauté the onion until transparent. Add the marjoram and sherry vinegar. Stir in the stock and the red wine, bring to a boil, and reduce by half. Strain the sauce and then gradually swirl in the butter. Season with salt and pepper to taste. Keep the sauce warm over a low heat.

5 Slice the rabbit and pheasant thinly against the grain. Pour the sauce onto six warm plates. Arrange a semi-circle of rabbit and a semi-circle of pheasant. In the centre place mushroom rice or sautéed forest mushrooms if liked.

——— •••• ———

SAUTÉED VENISON FILLETS AND RED CURRANT SAUCE

FOR SIX PEOPLE

4 tablespoons oil for sautéing
  whole venison fillets
  (tenderloin of venison),
  trimmed of fat and sprinkled
  with salt and pepper
30 g (1 oz) red currants
2 tablespoons sugar

1 teaspoon sherry vinegar
170 ml (generous $\frac{1}{4}$ pt) brown
  game stock
30 g (1 oz) butter, diced
salt and freshly ground white
  pepper to taste
red currants for garnish

1 Heat the oil in a frying pan and sauté the venison fillets over medium-high heat for about 3 minutes on each side. They should be brown outside and pink inside. Remove and keep warm on a covered plate.

2 Add the red currants, sugar, and sherry vinegar to the frying pan and sauté 3 to 4 minutes. Add the stock, bring to a boil, and reduce by half. Strain the sauce and then swirl in the butter. Season with salt and pepper to taste. Keep warm over a low flame.

3 Carve the venison fillets against the grain into long slices. Pour the redcurrant sauce onto six warm plates and arrange the venison slices in a circular pattern on the sauce. Garnish with red currants

●Serve with Viennese Red Cabbage, Courgette Tartlet, or Potato Strudel. The best time for fresh currants is around July.

——— •••• ———

MIXED GAME WITH A BLACKCURRANT SAUCE

FOR EIGHT PEOPLE

150 ml (¼ pt) oil for frying

700 g (1½ lbs) boned saddle of venison, cut into 6 portions and sprinkled with salt and pepper

700 g (1½ lbs) boned saddle of hare, cut into 6 portions and sprinkled with salt and pepper

6 boned pheasant breasts, sprinkled with salt and pepper

6 shallots, peeled and finely sliced

60 g (2 oz) blackcurrants for cooking

2 teaspoons sugar

2 teaspoons sherry vinegar

2 tablespoons cassis

225 ml (scant ½ pt) brown game stock

60 g (2 oz) butter, diced

salt and freshly ground pepper to taste

blackcurrants for garnish

1 Preheat the oven to 200°C/400°F/gas 6.

2 Heat 60 g (2 oz) oil in a frying pan and sauté the venison over medium-high heat until it is brown outside and pink inside. Remove and keep warm on a covered plate.

3 Add another 60 g (2 oz) oil to the frying pan and sauté the have until it is pink inside and brown outside. Remove and keep warm on a separate covered plate.

4 Heat 60 g (2 oz) oil in a separate ovenproof frying pan and sauté the pheasant breasts over medium-high heat for 3 to 4 minutes. Place the frying pan in the oven for 4 to 5 minutes. Remove and keep the pheasant warm on another covered plate.

5 In the frying pan used to cook the venison and the have, heat 30 g (1 oz) oil and sauté the shallots and the blackcurrants over medium heat for 3 to 4 minutes. Add the sugar. Then add the vinegar and cassis. Bring to a boil and reduce all of the liquid. Add the stock, bring to a boil, and reduce by half. Strain the sauce and then gradually swirl in the butter. Season with salt and pepper to taste and keep warm over a low heat.

6 Carve the meat against the grain into fine slices. Pour some sauce on each warm plate. Arrange the three meats in

triangles, forming an attractive star pattern. Whichever vegetable you choose should be served on a separate plate.

●A munificent feast of pheasant, venison, and hare, studded with tart fruit. Suitable accompaniments include: Viennese Red Cabbage, Champagne Cabbage, Dumplings in a Napkin, or glazed chestnuts. This noble fare calls for a smooth burgundy.

——— ••• ———

MEDALLIONS OF VENISON AND BLACK TRUFFLES SERVED WITH A PORT WINE SAUCE

FOR SIX PEOPLE

6 thin slices of fresh black truffle
2 tablespoons cognac
2 tablespoons Madeira
8 tablespoons oil for sautéing
1 kg (2 lbs) venison bones, chopped into small cubes with a cleaver (ask your game dealer to reserve and prepare the bones)
1 carrot, peeled and finely chopped

2 onions, finely chopped
1 leek (white portion only), well rinsed and coarsely chopped
stems of 1 bunch of parsley
225 ml (scant ½ pt) brown game stock
salt and freshly ground white pepper to taste
1.13 kg (2½ lbs) boned saddle of venison, cut into 12 medallions
30 g (1 oz) butter

1 Marinate the slices of truffle in the cognac and Madeira.

2 Heat 4 tablespoons oil in a frying pan and brown the chopped venison bones over high heat. Add all of the vegetables and the parsley stems and sauté until browned. Strain the truffles and add the Madeira and cognac to the frying pan. Add the game stock, bring to a boil, and reduce by half. Strain the sauce. Season with salt and pepper to taste. Keep warm over a low flame.

3 Next heat the remaining oil in a frying pan over medium-high heat and sauté the medallions of venison until medium-

rare, about 2 to 3 minutes on each side. Remove the meat and keep warm on a covered plate.

4 Cool the frying pan with some water and empty it. Pour the sauce into the frying pan and swirl in the butter.

5 Pour the sauce onto warm plates. Serve two medallions per person. One medallion should remain whole; slice the other in the middle and insert a marinated truffle. Place the medallion with the truffle over the other.

●Aromatic truffles give this venison a luxurious touch. Serve with Viennese Red Cabbage, Champagne Cabbage, Potato Croquettes Rolled in Almonds, or sautéed wild mushrooms. A truly sublime meal, especially with a bottle of smooth red wine.

CHAPTER 8

Beef, Lamb, and Pork

MEAT DISHES no longer have to be heavy, filling fare. Even the most calorie-conscious will crave these light beef, lamb, and pork dishes. Serve a light first course and then indulge in a hearty Viennese-style sirloin, a juicy pork chop given a lift with sorrel or capers, or fine lamb medallions smothered with wild mushrooms.

Austrians are known for their remarkable grilled beef dishes. The following are recipes for the most popular—Rostbraten, an impressive, easy, and particularly delicious way to treat your guests to a fine cut of sirloin.

———— •·• ————

ESTERHAZY-ROSTBRATEN
Esterhazy Sirloin of Beef

FOR SIX PEOPLE

10 white peppercorns
1 bay leaf
1 medium carrot, peeled and cut into thin strips
1 turnip, peeled and cut into thin strips
1 medium celeriac, cut into thin strips
70 g (2½ oz) clarified butter for sautéing
6 sirloin steaks, each weighing 200 g (7 oz)

1 medium onion, peeled and finely chopped
3 tablespoons cognac
225 ml (scant ½ pt) brown beef stock
8 tablespoons double cream
juice of 1 lemon
small knob butter
salt and freshly ground white pepper to taste
soured cream (optional)

1 Bring 1 litre (generous 1½ pts) of water to a boil. Add the peppercorns and bay leaf. Briefly and separately blanch the carrot, turnip, and celeriac. Refresh the vegetables in iced water and set aside. Reserve the vegetable stock resulting from the blanching and reduce to 5 tablespoons. Remove the bay leaf and peppercorns.

2 Heat 45 g (1½ oz) clarified butter in a frying pan and sauté the sirloin over medium-high heat until brown outside and medium-rare inside. Keep warm on a covered plate.

3 Degrease the pan. Heat 30 g (1 oz) clarified butter and sauté the onion over medium heat until golden. Add the cognac and reduce 3 to 5 minutes. Add the vegetable stock and again reduce 4 to 5 minutes over medium-high heat. Add the cream, lower heat to medium, and reduce by half.

4 Add the beef stock and once more reduce by half. Add the lemon juice and any meat juices from the covered plate. Drain the vegetables and stir them into the sauce. Swirl in the butter and season with salt and pepper to taste.

5 Place the meat on plates, topped with the sauce. The sirloin may be decorated with a swirled piping of soured cream, pressed through a piping bag.

●This traditional favourite was named after a family of aristocrats whose castles and churches are scattered throughout the Austrian province of Burgenland. The Esterhazys were known as music lovers, particularly as patrons of Haydn, Schubert, and Liszt. Many fine dishes in Austrian cuisine carry the Esterhazy name.

Esterhazy Sirloin is accompanied by a hearty sauce with vegetables. It may be served simply with Spaetzle or Château Potatoes.

————— •••• —————

ZWIEBELROSTBRATEN

FOR SIX PEOPLE

1 litre (generous 1½ pts) oil for frying the onions
3 onions, peeled and cut across into thin round slices
flour for the onions
45 g (1½ oz) clarified butter for sautéing
6 sirloin steaks, each weighing about 200 g (7 oz)

3 tablespoons cognac
3 tablespoons liquid from jar of pickled gherkins
225 ml (scant ½ pt) brown beef stock
15 g (½ oz) butter
1 tablespoon Dijon mustard
salt and freshly ground white pepper to taste

1 Heat the oil in a small deep fat frying pan. Meanwhile, dip the onion slices in some flour and pat to remove the excess. When the oil is hot, fry the onions until they are golden. Remove the onions from the oil, drain on kitchen paper, and keep warm on the stove top.

2 Heat the clarified butter in a frying pan and sauté the steaks slowly over medium-high heat until brown outside and medium-rare inside. Keep the steaks warm on a covered plate.

3 Degrease the frying pan by wiping it out with kitchen paper and add the cognac and gherkin liquid. Reduce almost all of the liquid. Add the beef stock and reduce by half.

4 Lower the heat. Whisk in the butter and mustard at the same time. Be sure to whisk well to avoid having clumps of mustard.

Add any meat juices from the steaks on the covered plate and stir well. Season with salt and pepper to taste.

5 Place the meat on warm plates. Pour the sauce over the meat and sprinkle with fried onions.

● A juicy sirloin steak topped with crunchy fried onions. The liquid from the jar of gherkins adds a subtle tang to the robust stock-cognac reduction sauce. This quick and easy dish is wonderful with seasonal vegetables and Rosti Potatoes (see Index) on the side. Try a full-bodied red wine. We suggest St-Laurent, Cabernet, or Austrian Pinot Noir.

————··————

VANILLA-ROSTBRATEN
Sirloin Steak with Garlic

FOR SIX PEOPLE

4 garlic cloves
15 g ($\frac{1}{2}$ oz) butter
45 g ($1\frac{1}{2}$ oz) clarified butter for sautéing
6 sirloin steaks, each weighing about 200 g (7 oz)
3 tablespoons Madeira

3 tablespoons liquid from jar of pickled gherkins
225 ml (scant $\frac{1}{2}$ pt) brown beef stock
$\frac{1}{4}$ bunch parsley, chopped
salt and freshly ground white pepper to taste

1 Peel the garlic cloves and blanch briefly in boiling water; then refresh in iced water. Chop the garlic in a food processor with the butter.

2 Heat the clarified butter and sauté the steaks over medium-high heat until brown outside and medium-rare inside. Remove and keep warm on a covered plate.

3 Degrease the pan by wiping it out with kitchen paper. Add the Madeira and gherkin liquid and reduce almost all of the liquid. Add the beef stock and reduce by three quarters.

4 Swirl in the prepared garlic butter with a whisk. Add any meat juices from the covered plate and reduce to a sauce

99

consistency. Add the chopped parsley, and season with salt and pepper to taste.

5 Place the steaks on warm plates and pour the sauce over them.

● Until the nineteenth century, spices from the East could be afforded only by the wealthy. The people made use of those seasonings which they could grow in their own gardens. Garlic came to be known in popular parlance as the 'poor man's vanilla.' Hence the misnomer of this Viennese speciality. Note that blanching the garlic and processing it with butter gives the sirloin sauce a mild but pungent flavour.

—— ·•· ——

GIRARDI-ROSTBRATEN
Girardi Sirloin Steak

FOR SIX PEOPLE

85 g (3 oz) clarified butter for sautéing

6 sirloin steaks, each weighing 200 g (7 oz)

6 tablespoons finely diced smoked ham

1 white onion, peeled and finely chopped

60 g (2 oz) finely diced mushrooms

6 tablespoons dry white wine

1 bay leaf

8 tablespoons double cream

180 ml (6 fl oz) brown beef stock

small knob butter

1 teaspoon Dijon mustard

½ bunch parsley, finely chopped

1 tablespoon capers, drained

salt and freshly ground white pepper to taste

soured cream (optional)

1 Heat 60 g (2 oz) clarified butter in a frying pan and sauté the sirloin over medium-high heat until brown outside and medium-rare inside. Remove and set aside on a covered plate.

2 Degrease the frying pan by wiping it out with kitchen paper, add the remaining clarified butter, and sauté the smoked ham 2 to 3 minutes over medium-high heat. Add the onions and sauté until golden. Add the mushrooms and sauté 4 to 5 minutes. Add the white wine and reduce almost all of the liquid.

3 Add the bay leaf, cream, and stock, and reduce to a sauce consistency. Swirl in the butter and whisk in the mustard. Do not allow the sauce to boil again or the mustard will have a bitter taste. Stir in the parsley, any meat juices from the covered plate, the capers, and salt and pepper to taste. Remove the bay leaf.

4 Place the meat on six warm plates, topped with the sauce. The dish may be decorated with soured cream piped through a piping bag.

●Alexander Girardi was born in Graz in 1850, the son of Italian immigrants. He began working as an itinerant locksmith, but soon turned to the stage, acting in provincial theatres. He was 'discovered' in 1870 and became one of the most popular actors in Vienna, so admired that the Viennese named one of their favourite dishes for him.

The Girardi-Rostbraten is accompanied by a light cream sauce scented with bay leaf and enriched with diced smoked ham and mushrooms. Serve with seasonal vegetables and buttered noodles. Open a bottle of Cabernet, Merlot, or Pinot Noir St-Laurent.

101

TAFELSPITZ

FOR SIX PEOPLE

1 medium carrot	½ bunch parsley
1 medium turnip	1 bay leaf
½ celeriac	15 black peppercorns
1 stick of celery	1.8 kg (4 lb) rib of beef on the
1 medium onion	bone (the meat on the bone
1 leek (both white and green	should be 6.5 cm (2½″) thick
parts), well rinsed and	and not too fatty)
trimmed	

1 Peel the vegetables and cut them all into 2.5 cm (1″) slices.

2 Half fill a large saucepan with water and bring to a boil. Add the vegetables and seasonings and bring to a second boil.

3 Add the beef, lower the flame, and slowly simmer for 2 to 3 hours, until the meat is tender.

4 When the meat is done, remove the bone and carve against the grain into thick slices.

●Ribs of beef are slowly simmered with a bouquet of vegetables to a special tenderness. Tafelspitz is a glory of Austrian cuisine, proving that simple, time-honoured fare can be the most memorable. Because it requires little attention, practically cooking itself over a two- to three-hour period, Tafelspitz is well suited to both family dinners and entertaining. The succulent boiled beef is particularly wonderful served with its two traditional accompaniments, chive sauce and horseradish-apple sauce. The recipes for these fresh-tasting relishes immediately follow the Tafelspitz. All that's needed for a perfect meal is buttered new potatoes with a sprinkling of dill and some creamed spinach. Any other creamed vegetable will be equally good. It is interesting to note that the Viennese invariably serve a light white wine with this meat dish. We suggest a Pinot Blanc, Riesling, Chardonnay, or Sauvignon Blanc.

———— ••• ————

TRADITIONAL SAUCES FOR THE TAFELSPITZ CHIVE SAUCE

MAKES 680 ML (1¼ PTS)

yolks of 6 hard-boiled eggs
4 tablespoons milk
5 slices of white bread without
  the crusts
225 ml (scant ½ pt) mayonnaise
8 tablespoons soured cream

6 tablespoons white vinegar
  (about)
salt and freshly ground white
  pepper to taste
3 bunches of chives, finely
  chopped

1 In a blender or food processor, combine the egg yolks, milk, and bread until smooth.

2 Stir in the mayonnaise and soured cream. Add white vinegar to taste and season with salt and pepper to taste. Stir in the chives.

3 Serve in a bowl to accompany the Tafelspitz.

———•••———

HORSERADISH-APPLE SAUCE

MAKES 680 ML (1¼ PTS)

6 apples, peeled, halved, and
  cored
1 whole clove
8 tablespoons dry white wine

12 tablespoons freshly grated
  horseradish
juice of 1 lemon
1 tablspoon sugar

1 Cook the apples in 680 ml (1¼ pts) water with the clove and white wine until tender.

2 Refresh the apples in iced water and then beat until smooth.

3 Stir in the horseradish, lemon juice, and sugar.

4 Serve in a bowl to accompany the Tafelspitz.

———•••———

VIENNESE ROAST TENDERLOIN OF BEEF IN CREAM SAUCE

FOR SIX PEOPLE

700 g (1½ lbs) whole fillet of beef, with fat removed
115 g (4 oz) pork back fat, cut into strips
225 ml (scant ½ pt) soured cream
1 tablespoon Dijon mustard
1 tablespoon capers, drained
Pinch of dried thyme

Juice of 1 lemon
45 g (1½ oz) butter for frying
1 medium onion, diced
225 ml (scant ½ pt) double cream
425 ml (¾ pt) brown beef stock
salt and freshly ground white pepper to taste

1 Preheat the oven to 200°C/400°F/gas 6.

2 Lard the fillet by making small lengthways incisions in the beef and inserting the strips of back fat.

3 In a bowl, mix the soured cream, mustard, capers, thyme, and lemon juice.

4 Heat the butter in a frying pan and brown the fillet over medium-high heat on both sides. Transfer to a roasting tin and place in the oven for 25 minutes.

5 Meanwhile, fry the onion in the same frying pan until golden. Add the double cream, bring to a boil, and reduce by half. Add the beef stock and again reduce by half.

6 Remove from the heat and stir in the soured cream mixture. Season with salt and pepper to taste and set aside.

7 Remove the beef from the oven and carve against the grain into 2.5 cm (1″) slices. Pour the sauce on six warm plates and arrange two slices of beef on the sauce for each serving.

●We find that larding makes this beef even more succulent and tender. Capers add a special note to the smooth cream sauce. Serve with seasonal vegetables and lightly buttered noodles.

——— • • • ———

FILET MIGNON WITH BEAUJOLAIS SAUCE AND A VARIETY OF MARINATED MUSHROOMS

FOR SIX PEOPLE

100 g (3½ oz) butter
2 medium onions, thinly sliced
8 tablespoons Beaujolais
300 ml (½ pt) brown beef stock
6 black peppercorns
2 bay leaves
20 g (¾ oz) sliced fresh shiitake mushrooms
20 g (¾ oz) fresh enoki mushrooms (tiny Japanese mushrooms)
20 g (¾ oz) fresh chanterelles, rinsed, dried on kitchen paper and torn in half by hand
4 shallots, peeled and minced
pinch of dried thyme
2 garlic cloves, peeled
1 tablespoon tarragon vinegar
salt and freshly ground white pepper to taste
6 filet mignons, each weighing 180 g (6 oz)
3 tablespoons oil for sautéing

1 Heat 60 g (2 oz) butter in a saucepan and brown the sliced onions over medium heat.

2 Add the Beaujolais, bring to a boil, and reduce almost all of the liquid.

3 Add the beef stock, peppercorns, and bay leaves, and reduce by half. Strain and keep warm.

4 Heat 30 g (1 oz) butter in a frying pan over medium heat and brown all of the mushrooms. Add the shallots and brown.

5 Add the thyme. Spear the garlic cloves on a kitchen fork and stir in the pan for 2 to 3 minutes.

6 Add the tarragon vinegar and salt and pepper to taste. Remove from the heat and allow the mushrooms to marinate while you prepare the fillets.

7 Preheat the oven to 200°C/400°F/gas 6.

8 Sprinkle the fillets with salt and pepper.

9 Pour the oil in a large ovenproof frying pan or flameproof gratin dish and heat well. Sauté the fillets over medium-high heat on both sides to sear the meat, then finish cooking them in the oven for 6 to 8 minutes, in the same pan or dish.

10 While the fillets are in the oven, bring the sauce to a boil once more and swirl in the remaining butter. Heat the mushrooms through a second time.

11 Pour the sauce on to six warm plates and place the fillets in the centre, surrounded by marinated mushrooms.

●The supreme flavour of wild mushrooms gives this otherwise traditional dish a lavish distinction. A tip for preparation: instead of adding garlic directly to the mushrooms and overpowering their aroma, spear whole garlic cloves and stir them through the mushrooms for a few minutes. Perfect with Potato Strudel. The same Beaujolais used for cooking should accompany the dish at table.

————— ••• —————

LAMB MEDALLIONS WITH MINT SAUCE

FOR SIX PEOPLE

about 115 g (4 oz) clarified butter for sautéing
12 lamb medallions, about 2.5 cm (1″) thick
6 shallots, peeled and finely diced
leaves of 1 bunch fresh peppermint (reserve some nice leaves for garnishing each plate)

2 cloves garlic, chopped
2 tablespoons red wine
2 tablespoons clear mint liqueur (try a peppermint schnapps)
170 ml (generous ¼ pt) lamb stock
pinch of dried thyme
salt and freshly ground white pepper to taste

1 Heat 45 g (1½ oz) clarified butter in a frying pan and sauté six of the lamb medallions over medium-high heat on both sides until they are browned outside and pink inside. Remove and keep warm on a covered plate. Add another 45 g (1½ oz) clarified butter and repeat with the remaining medallions.

2 Heat 30 g (1 oz) clarified butter in the frying pan and sauté the shallots over medium heat for 3 to 4 minutes, until they are transparent. Next add the mint leaves and garlic. Sauté 3 to 4 minutes.

3 Add the red wine and mint liqueur. Reduce almost all of the liquid.

4 Add the lamb stock and reduce to a sauce consistency.

5 Strain the sauce. Season with the thyme and salt and pepper to taste.

6 Slice the lamb medallions diagonally against the grain. Pour the sauce on to six warm plates. Arrange the slices of lamb in a circular pattern over the sauce. Decorate with mint leaves in the centre. Arrange seasonal vegetables around the meat.

●This is an impressive Easter dish. Wild rice and a full-bodied, elegant red wine are appropriate.

LAMB CUTLETS WITH POMMERY MUSTARD SAUCE

FOR SIX PEOPLE

6–9 tablespoons olive oil for sautéing
24 lamb cutlets (4 per person)
8 shallots, peeled and finely diced
8 tablespoons red wine
1 clove garlic, peeled and crushed
225 ml (scant ½ pt) lamb stock or brown veal stock
10 black peppercorns
1 bay leaf
1 tablespoon Pommery mustard
225 g (8 oz) butter, diced
2 pinches of dried thyme
salt and freshly ground white pepper to taste
3 medium courgettes, cut into thin strips
2 tomatoes, skin and seeds removed, and diced

1 Heat 3 tablespoons olive oil in a frying pan and sauté the lamb cutlets, 6 at a time, on both sides over medium-high heat, until brown outside and pink inside. Remove and keep warm on a covered plate. Repeat with the remaining cutlets, adding more oil as necessary.

2 Add the shallots to the frying pan and sauté until golden. Add the red wine and garlic and reduce almost all of the liquid. Add the lamb stock, peppercorns, and bay leaf. Reduce to a sauce consistency.

3 Strain the sauce into another pan. slowly whisk in the Pommery mustard. Over a very low flame, gradually swirl in the butter. Do not allow the sauce to boil again. Add a pinch a thyme and season with salt and pepper to taste.

4 Heat 3 tablespoons olive oil in a frying pan and sauté the courgettes briefly over medium-high heat, about 1 minute. Add the tomato and again sauté briefly until tender. Season with a pinch of thyme.

5 Place four cutlets on each plate in a circular pattern. Pour the sauce in the middle and arrange the vegetables over the sauce.

●Serve with a light salad, mushrooms, and crusty bread.

LOIN OF LAMB WITH FOREST MUSHROOMS AND BASIL LEAVES

FOR SIX PEOPLE

150 ml (¼ pt) olive oil for sautéing

60 g (2 oz) fresh chanterelles, rinsed, dried on kitchen paper, and torn in half by hand

60 g (2 oz) fresh cèpes, rinsed, drained, patted dry with kitchen paper, and cut in thin slices

45 g (1½ oz) fresh shiitake, thinly sliced

45 g (1½ oz) fresh pleurots (wild mushrooms), thinly sliced

8 shallots, peeled and finely diced

pinch of dried thyme

4 cloves garlic, peeled

1 kg (2 lbs) boned loin of lamb, fat removed, cut into 6 portions

salt and freshly ground white pepper to taste

12 large fresh basil leaves

225 g (8 oz) caul fat

24 stoned black olives, finely diced, plus 2 tablespoons liquid from the jar of olives

225 ml (scant ½ pt) lamb stock

1 Preheat the oven to 220°C/425°C/gas 7.

2 Heat 4 tablespoons olive oil in a frying pan and sauté all of the mushrooms over medium-high heat for 7 to 8 minutes. Add half of the shallots and sauté until golden. Add a pinch of thyme.

3 Spear the garlic cloves on a kitchen fork and stir through the mushrooms for 2 minutes. Reserve the garlic. Remove the mushrooms and shallots and allow to cool.

4 Heat 3 tablespoons olive oil in the same frying pan. Sprinkle the meat with salt and pepper to taste. Quickly brown the meat over medium-high heat for about 1 minute on each side. Remove and allow to cool.

5 Place some mushrooms over each portion of lamb and top with 2 basil leaves. Seal each portion in caul fat by wrapping it like a present, tucking the fat under each end securely.

6 Heat the remaining olive oil in an ovenproof frying pan or flameproof gratin dish and sauté the prepared meat over medium-high heat for 1 minute on each side. Transfer the frying pan or gratin dish to the oven and roast for 3 to 4 minutes. Keep warm on a covered plate.

7 In the frying pan or gratin dish in which the lamb has been roasted, add the remaining shallots and sauté over medium-high heat until golden. Add the whole garlic and brown. Add the sliced olives and olive juice and reduce almost all of the liquid. Add the lamb stock and reduce by half. Remove the garlic.

8 Cut each portion of lamb into five slices. Arrange the slices on warm plates. Pour the sauce over the meat.

●Serve with Courgette Tartlets and a bottle of Cabernet Sauvignon.

———— •••• ————

PORK MEDALLIONS IN SORREL SAUCE

FOR SIX PEOPLE

Clarified butter for sautéing
1 kg (2 lb) trimmed pork tenderloin, cut into 18 medallions (3 per person)
4 shallots, peeled and finely diced
2 garlic cloves, peeled
6 tablespoons red wine vinegar
1 bunch sorrel, rinsed, dried, and finely chopped

225 ml (scant $\frac{1}{2}$ pt) double cream
4 tablespoons pork stock
15 g ($\frac{1}{2}$ oz) butter
salt and freshly ground white pepper to taste
$\frac{1}{2}$ bunch sorrel, rinsed, drained, and finely sliced for garnishing

1 Heat 60 g (2 oz) clarified butter in a frying pan and sauté the medallions of pork in batches of six, adding extra butter as necessary. Cook over medium-high heat for 3 to 4 minutes on each side. Remove and keep warm on a covered plate.

2 Degrease the frying pan by wiping it out with a paper towel and heat 30 g (1 oz) fresh clarified butter. Add the shallots and garlic cloves and sauté over medium-high heat until golden. Add the red wine vinegar and reduce by half.

3 Add the chopped sorrel and double cream. Again reduce by half.

4 Add the pork stock and allow to reduce for 4 to 5 minutes. Strain the sauce into another frying pan and swirl in the butter. Season with salt and white pepper to taste.

5 Place the pork medallions on warm plates and pour some sauce over them. Arrange the sliced sorrel near the medallions.

●The light sharpness of fresh sorrel is a geat complement for pork. Easy, and delicious—we particularly like this dish served with Truffle Crêpes and a fresh vegetable.

———•••———

PORK CHOPS WITH CAPER SAUCE

FOR SIX PEOPLE

1 garlic clove, peeled
8 tablespoons olive oil, plus 6 tablespoons olive oil for sautéing
12 pork chops, each weighing 115–150 g (4–5 oz)
2 teaspoons dry red wine
225 ml (scant ½ pt) pork stock

juice of 1 lemon
4 tablespoons double cream
2 tablespoons capers, drained
dash of caper juice
½ bunch fresh parsley, chopped
salt and freshly ground white pepper to taste

1 Pass the garlic clove through a garlic press, then mix with the 8 tablespoons olive oil, or process together until smooth.

2 Brush the pork chops on both sides with the garlic-oil mixture.

3 Heat 3 tablespoons oil in a frying pan over medium-high heat and sauté six of the chops for about 5 to 6 minutes on each side. Lift out the chops, drain, and keep warm on a covered plate. Add the remaining oil and repeat with the remaining chops.

4 Degrease the frying pan by wiping it out with kitchen paper. Add the red wine and stock. Reduce to a sauce consistency. Add the lemon juice and cream. Strain the sauce and return to the pan. Add the capers and a dash of caper juice. Stir in the parsley. Season with salt and pepper to taste.

5 Arrange the chops on six warm plates and spoon the sauce over them.

●An easy, last-minute dish. Serve with green beans and Lyonnaise Potatoes. Any dry, light Chardonnay goes well with pork.

BRAISED PORK FILLETS IN WHITE CABBAGE

FOR SIX PEOPLE

6 pork fillets (from the
  tenderloin), each weighing
  225 g (8 oz) trimmed of all fat
salt and freshly ground black
  pepper to taste
vegetable oil
2 cloves garlic, peeled and
  crushed
1 medium onion, sliced
$\frac{1}{2}$ large carrot, peeled and diced
$\frac{1}{4}$ celeriac, diced
a few stems of parsley
1 medium head white cabbage
1 tablespoon caraway seeds
1 bay leaf
white peppercorns
dash of white vinegar
3 tablespoons olive oil for
  sautéing

225 g (8 oz) bacon, chopped
8 tablespoons dry white wine
8 tablespoons pork stock
8 tablespoons bouillon

MUSHROOM MOUSSE
450 g (1 lb) cultivated
  mushrooms, cleaned and
  chopped
10 shallots, peeled and chopped
60 g (2 oz) butter
2 cloves garlic, peeled and
  minced
juice of 1 lemon
225 ml (scant $\frac{1}{2}$ pt) double cream
1 egg yolk
salt and freshly ground white
  pepper to taste

1 Season the pork fillets with salt and pepper. Place them in a dish, cover with oil, and cover with layers of the garlic, vegetables, and parsley. Cover and allow to marinate for 12 hours.

2 Take off 8–10 large leaves from the cabbage and reserve. Chop the rest of the leaves and set aside. Discard the core.

3 Bring 1 litre (generous $1\frac{1}{2}$ pts) water to a boil. Add the caraway, bay leaf, peppercorns, and vinegar.

4 Blanch the 8–10 large cabbage leaves, remove, and refresh in iced water. Drain the cabbage leaves on kitchen paper.

5 For the mousse, sauté the mushrooms and shallots in the butter over medium heat. When the shallots are golden, add the garlic. Add the lemon juice and cream.

6 Purée in a food processor and return to the pan. Bring to a boil and reduce to a firm consistency.

7 Remove from the heat, stir in the egg yolk, season with salt and pepper to taste, and allow to cool.

8 Preheat the oven to 150°C/300°F/gas 2.

9 Remove the meat from the marinade and let the oil drip off. Strain the vegetables from the marinade and set aside.

10 Heat the oil in a frying pan and sauté the fillets over high heat until golden on both sides. Remove and allow to cool.

11 Spread out the large cabbage leaves and cover with mushroom mousse. Place the fillets on top and roll up the cabbage leaves. Tie tightly with string.

12 Over medium-high heat, sauté the chopped bacon for 4 to 5 minutes in a large ovenproof casserole with a lid. Add the vegetables and chopped cabbage from the marinade and sauté for 4 to 5 minutes. Pour in the white wine and layer the fillets over the vegetables. Cover with the pork stock and bouillon. Cover the pot and place it in the preheated oven. Braise for 40 minutes.

13 Remove the fillets. Reduce the remaining stock to a sauce consistency and strain it.

14 Slice each fillet of pork and arrange it in a circular pattern on an individual plate. Place the vegetables alongside and drizzle the sauce over all.

●This is somewhat complicated but is especially rewarding on a chill winter's night.

─── ·•· ───

MEDALLIONS OF PORK WITH A BEER AND CARAWAY SAUCE

FOR SIX PEOPLE

2 cloves garlic, peeled
425 ml ($\frac{3}{4}$ pt) olive oil
6 tenderloins of pork, each weighing 200 g (7 oz), cut into 18 medallions (3 per person) (reserve trimmed fat and meat for making the sauce; cut the trimmings into 2.5 cm (1″) cubes)
1 medium carrot, peeled and finely diced
1 celeriac, finely diced
1 stick of celery, finely diced
1 medium onion, finely diced
caraway seeds
350 ml (generous $\frac{1}{2}$ pt) beer
4 tablespoons pork stock (see Index)
salt and freshly ground white pepper to taste

1 Purée the garlic cloves with the olive oil until smooth.

2 Place the pork medallions in a dish, cover with the garlic oil, and add the vegetables and a sprinkling of caraway seed. Cover and allow to marinate 12 hours or overnight.

3 Sauté the reserved cubed meat and fat in a frying pan. Add the vegetables from the marinade and sauté. Add the beer and reduce by half. Season with caraway seeds to taste. Add 4 tablespoons water and the stock and simmer, uncovered, over low heat for 1$\frac{1}{2}$ hours.

4 Remove the medallions from the garlic oil and pat them dry. Brush them on both sides with the garlic oil. Heat the remaining garlic oil in a frying pan and sauté the medallions over medium-high heat for 3 to 4 minutes on each side. Remove and set aside on a covered plate.

5 Degrease the frying pan by wiping it out with kitchen paper. Strain the sauce into the frying pan, add the pork medallions, and heat through without allowing the sauce to boil.

6 Arrange the medallions on six plates and spoon sauce over each.

●If you wish, marinate the pork overnight. Serve this robust winter fare with Beans and Bacon. Accompany with the same beer used for cooking.

Chapter 9

Vegetables

THE BEST side dishes are often the simplest—a colourful array of fresh vegetables, a fine salad, moulded white or wild rice. There are times, however, when you will want to complete your meal with something a little more special. Here we give the potato, much loved in Austria, particular attention. This simple vegetable is subject to ingenious transformations, making it compatible with dishes ranging from the unassuming to the elegant. Inexpensive and surprisingly nutritious, the potato can be enjoyed in many delectable guises.

———··———

POTATO STRUDEL

FOR SIX PEOPLE

450 g (1 lb) Maris Piper or King Edward potatoes
vegetable oil for the baking sheet
350 g (12 oz) puff pastry (readymade is acceptable)
4 tablespoons olive oil for sautéing

450 g (1 lb) onions, finely sliced
1 clove garlic, peeled
dash of marjoram
salt and freshly ground white pepper to taste
2 egg yolks mixed with a few drops of water
4 tablespoons double cream

1 Peel the potatoes and cut into finger-thick slices. Soak the slices in cold water.

2 Preheat the oven to 200°C/400°F/gas 6. Grease a baking sheet with oil.

3 Roll out the puff pastry to 75 mm ($\frac{1}{4}$″) thick. Cut into two pieces, one slightly larger than the other. Place the smaller half on the baking sheet.

4 Heat the olive oil in a frying pan, add the onions, and sauté over medium-high heat until golden. Drain the potatoes, add them, and stir for 3 minutes. Spear the garlic clove on a kitchen fork and stir it through the mixture for 1 minute. Season with marjoram, salt, and white pepper to taste. Remove from the heat and allow to cool to room temperature.

5 Spread the mixture on the pastry bottom, leaving 2.5 cm (1") free on all sides. Brush the sides with egg yolk, cover with the larger sheet of pastry, and seal. Brush the pastry top with the remaining egg yolk.

6 Bake the potato strudel for 15 minutes. Remove from the oven and let it cool for 5 minutes on the baking sheet. Cut 2.5 cm (1")-thick strip of dough from the top of the strudel and pour in the cream.

7 Lower the oven to 95°C/200°F/gas $\frac{1}{4}$ and bake the strudel for another 10 minutes, to allow the cream to thicken.

8 Remove, slice, and serve warm.

● Served with a good soup, this side dish becomes a rich, earthy meal in itself.

———··———

SPRING ONION POTATOES

FOR SIX PEOPLE

450 g (1 lb) Maris Piper or King Edward potatoes, peeled
1 egg yolk
pinch of grated nutmeg
salt and freshly ground white pepper to taste

1 bunch spring onions (white portion only), sliced
4 tablespoons butter for sautéing
1 tablespoon olive oil for sautéing

1 Preheat the oven to 95°C/200°F/gas $\frac{1}{4}$.

2 In a pot of cold water, bring the potatoes to a boil, cook until tender, and then mash them.

3 Place the mashed potatoes in a flameproof casserole over low heat. Stir in the egg yolk. Season with nutmeg, salt, and pepper. Transfer the casserole to the oven for 10 minutes.

117

4 Over medium heat, sauté the spring onions in butter for 4 to 5 minutes and mix them into the potatoes. Form little cylinders or ovals.

5 Heat the olive oil in a frying pan and sauté the spring onion potatoes over medium-high heat until golden on all sides.

6 Drain on kitchen paper and serve warm with a grinding of fresh pepper.

● This delicious and original dish can be served with a wide variety of meats and poultry.

—— • • • ——

DUCHESSE POTATOES

FOR SIX PEOPLE

700 g (1½ lbs) Maris Piper or
   King Edward potatoes
2 egg yolks

salt and freshly ground white
   pepper to taste
¼ teaspoon grated nutmeg
butter for the baking sheet

1 Quarter the potatoes (unpeeled) and boil until tender. Allow to cool, peel, and mash the potatoes.

2 Preheat the oven to 95°C/200°F/gas ¼.

3 Mix the mashed potatoes and one of the egg yolks. Season with salt, pepper, and the nutmeg. Place the mixture in the oven for 10 minutes. Remove.

4 Preheat the oven to 200°C/400°F/gas 6.

5 Butter a baking sheet. Place the potato mixture in a piping bag fitted with a large rosette nozzle and pipe 7.5 cm (3″) high swirls onto the baking sheet. Beat the remaining egg yolk with a few drops of water and brush the top of each swirl with it. Bake for 5 minutes, until the tops are browned.

● All you need is a piping bag to make these delicate potato rosettes—a simple and elegant dish.

TRUFFLE CREPES

FOR SIX PEOPLE

700 g (1½ lbs) Maris Piper or King Edward potatoes
1 egg yolk
salt and freshly ground white pepper to taste
small knob of butter for sautéing

3 shallots, peeled and finely diced
1 tablespoon truffles, finely diced
1 tablespoon truffle juice
3 tablespoons olive oil for sautéing

1 Quarter the unpeeled potatoes, and boil until tender. Allow to cool, then peel and mash.

2 Preheat the oven to 95°C/200°F/gas ¼.

3 Combine the mashed potatoes and egg yolk. Season with salt and pepper. Place the mixture in the oven for 10 minutes.

4 Meanwhile, melt the butter in a frying pan and sauté the shallots over medium-high heat for 4 to 5 minutes. Stir in the truffles and add the truffle juice. Reduce by half.

5 Stir the shallots and truffles into the potatoes. Form twelve flat oval crêpe shapes. Heat the olive oil in the frying pan and sauté the crêpes over medium-high heat until golden.

6 Serve warm.

● An inventive marriage of the faithful potato and the elegant truffle. A worldly indulgence.

———— •●• ————

ROSTI POTATOES

FOR SIX PEOPLE

450 g (1 lb) Maris Piper or King Edward potatoes
2–3 tablespoons vegetable oil
1 medium onion, chopped

salt and freshly ground white pepper to taste
4 tablespoons finely chopped parsley for garnishing

1 Boil the potatoes in their skins for 20 minutes. Peel them and grate them coarsely.

2 Heat the oil in a large frying pan until very hot.

3 Add the onion and cook over medium heat until golden.

4 Sprinkle the potatoes over the onions, cover the frying pan, and cook 10 minutes, shaking the frying pan occasionally.

5 Turn the potato-onion pancake in one piece: cover the frying pan with a platter and flip them over together so the pancake comes out whole on the plate. Slide the pancake back into the frying pan, brown side up. Cover and cook another 10 minutes, until crisp.

6 Garnish with the chopped parsley and serve.

——— ••• ———

CHATEAU POTATOES

FOR SIX PEOPLE

18 small red-skinned potatoes
3–4 tablespoons vegetable oil

4 tablespoons brown veal stock

1 Turn the potatoes against a sharp paring knife, cutting them into 6-sided cylinders.

2 Blanch the potatoes in boiling water and drain. Heat the oil in a large frying pan and fry the potatoes over medium heat until brown.

3 Remove the potatoes from the oil and place in a saucepan with the stock. Cook over medium heat until the liquid is reduced by half, about 7 to 8 minutes.

4 Cover and keep warm until ready to serve.

● A brief simmering in veal stock gives a rewarding flavour to Château and Lyonnaise potatoes.

———··———

LYONNAISE POTATOES

FOR SIX PEOPLE

450 g (1 lb) potatoes
3–4 tablespoons olive oil for
   sautéing
450 g (1 lb) onions, sliced

dash of thyme
1 clove garlic, peeled
3–4 tablespoons brown veal
   stock

1 Boil the potatoes in their skins for about 15 minutes. Allow to cool, then peel and cut into 5 cm (2")-thick slices.

2 In a large frying pan heat some of the oil over medium heat and sauté the onions until golden. Slowly stir in the potatoes, adding more oil if necessary, and sprinkle with the thyme. Spear the garlic clove on a kitchen fork and stir through the mixture several times. Cook for 10 minutes, until the potatoes form a golden crust.

3 Pour in the veal stock, heat through, and serve.

● A variation on the preceding recipe, these potatoes are touched with a hint of garlic, as well as the traditional onions.

———··———

POTATO NOODLES

FOR SIX PEOPLE

450 g (1 lb) Maris Piper or King
   Edward potatoes
100 g (3½ oz) flour
1 egg

½ teaspoon grated nutmeg
⅛ teaspoon salt
4 tablespoons olive oil for
   sautéing

1 Boil the unpeeled potatoes until tender and refrigerate over-night. The next day, peel the potatoes and force them through a fine sieve.

2 Mix the sieved potatoes, flour, and egg to form a dough. Season with the nutmeg and salt. Roll the dough into a finger-thick cylindrical shape and cut it into 2.5 cm (1″) long sections. Roll each section into noodles thick in the middle and tapering at the ends.

3 Bring 2 litres (3¼ pts) of water to a boil. Add the noodles and simmer for about 5 minutes, until the noodles rise to the surface. Remove the noodles with a slotted spoon and refresh in iced water.

4 Heat the olive oil in a frying pan and sauté the potato noodles over medium-high heat until golden brown.

● Austrians living abroad sigh with remembered pleasure at the mention of potato noodles, a beloved regional speciality of Styria and Tyrol. Try these once and you will share the enthusiasm, especially with meat dishes.

———— •••• ————

POTATO CROQUETTES ROLLED IN ALMONDS

FOR SIX PEOPLE

450 g (1 lb) Maris Piper or King
  Edward potatoes, peeled
1 egg yolk
salt and freshly ground white
  pepper to taste
flour

2 eggs mixed with 4 tablespoons
  milk
60 g (2 oz) ground blanched
  almonds
oil for deep frying

1 Cook the potatoes in boiling, salted water until tender. Allow them to cool and mash them.

2 Preheat the oven to the lowest possible setting.

3 Mix the mashed potatoes and the egg yolk. Season with salt and pepper. Place in the oven for 10 minutes. Allow to cool.

4 Form the potato mixture into 10 cm (2") cylinders. Roll in the flour, dip in the egg-milk mixture, and then roll in the almonds. Deep-fry in very hot oil until golden brown.

● A variation on the familiar croquettes, these potatoes are rolled in ground almonds rather than breadcrumbs. The contrast of texture is incredibly delicious!

———·•·———

SIMPLE POTATO CROQUETTES

These are prepared in the same way as the previous recipe, substituting breadcrumbs for the almonds.

———·•·———

123

POTATO ROULADE

FOR SIX PEOPLE

450 g (1 lb) potatoes, unpeeled
1 egg
150 g (5 oz) flour, plus flour for rolling out dough
small knob of butter
4 shallots, peeled and diced
115 g (4 oz) finely diced cooked ham

60 g (2 oz) diced mushrooms
2 tablespoons finely chopped basil
olive oil
salt and freshly ground white pepper to taste

1 Boil the unpeeled potatoes until tender. Allow to cool, peel, and mash.

2 Mix the mashed potatoes, egg, and flour to form a dough. Allow to rest for 15 minutes.

3 Heat the butter in a frying pan and sauté the shallots, ham, mushrooms, and basil. Allow to cool.

4 Sprinkle flour on a tabletop and roll out the dough into a 1.25 cm ($\frac{1}{2}$")-thick square. Cover with the cooled ham mixture, leaving a 2.5 cm (1") border clear all the way round. Roll up the dough like a Swiss roll and carefully seal the ends by pinching and twisting the dough.

5 Roll the roulade in buttered greaseproof paper cut 10 cm (4") longer than the roulade. Tie the ends of the greaseproof paper with string. Place the roulade in a saucepan of boiling water and simmer, uncovered, for 20–30 minutes.

6 Take out the roulade, refresh in iced water, and remove the parchment. Cut the roulade into 1.25 cm ($\frac{1}{2}$") slices.

7 Heat a little olive oil in a frying pan, preferably non-stick and gently sauté the roulade until golden on both sides.

● Beautiful when sliced, our roulade holds a luscious mixture of sautéed ham, shallots, mushrooms, and fragrant basil. Unsurpassed with game, or a hearty meal in itself (serving four) with a good glass of wine.

SPAETZLE

FOR SIX PEOPLE

300 g (10 oz) flour
8 tablespoons milk
3 eggs, beaten

salt and freshly ground white
pepper to taste
60 g (2 oz) butter

1 Mix the flour, milk, and eggs to form a dough.

2 Season with salt and pepper and process in a spaetzle machine. If you don't wish to purchase a spaetzle machine, you can try pushing the spaetzle dough through a colander into the boiling water.

3 Bring a large saucepan of water to a boil. Drop in the spaetzle and return to a boil. Remove the spaetzle and refresh in iced water. Drain and pat dry with kitchen paper.

4 Sauté the spaetzle in the butter in a large frying pan over medium-high heat without browning, for 4 to 5 minutes.

5 Serve immediately.

● A spaetzle machine looks like a large cheese grater. These machines can be found at good kitchenware shops and departments. Spaetzle are wonderful for absorbing rich sauces and can be served with almost any sauced dish. Spaetzle are considered the pasta of central Europe, a mainstay of Austrian meals.

DUMPLINGS IN A NAPKIN
Serviettenknödel

FOR SIX PEOPLE

15 stale white rolls, approximately 60 g (2 oz) each
425 ml (¾ pt) milk
3 eggs, separated, at room temperature

115 g (4 oz) butter, melted, plus butter for the napkin
salt and freshly ground white pepper to taste
¼ teaspoon grated nutmeg
olive oil for sautéing

1 Remove the crusts from the rolls and crumble the inside of the rolls. Soak the bread in the milk.

2 In an electric blender, mix the egg yolks and the melted butter until frothy. Stir this mixture into the rolls and milk. Season with salt and pepper to taste and the nutmeg.

3 Whisk the egg whites until stiff peaks form and carefully fold into the bread mixture.

4 Bring a large saucepan of water to a boil. Spread out a white linen napkin and butter it lightly. Form the bread mixture into a 12.5 cm (12″)-thick cylinder and place it on the lower end of the napkin. Roll up the napkin and tie the ends securely with string.

5 Place the napkin in the boiling water and simmer for 25-30 minutes. Refresh in iced water, untie, and slice the dumpling. Discard the end slices.

6 Heat a little olive oil in a frying pan, preferably non-stick, and sauté the dumplings over medium-high heat for 1 to 2 minutes on each side before serving.

● Knödel, or dumplings, are a popular dish in Austria. Try this sophisticated variation cooked in a white linen napkin.

———— •●• ————

MUSHROOM RICE

FOR SIX PEOPLE

60 g (2 oz) butter
1 onion, finely diced
225 g (8 oz) mushrooms, cleaned
  and sliced
425 ml ($\frac{3}{4}$ pt) bouillon or
  chicken stock

200 g (7 oz) raw rice
salt and freshly ground black
  pepper to taste
$\frac{1}{2}$ bunch parsley, finely chopped

1 Heat the butter in a large saucepan and sauté the onion until transparent. Add the mushrooms, and sauté.

2 Pour in the bouillon, stir in the rice, cover, and cook over low heat for 20 minutes.

3 Uncover and continue cooking for 5 minutes. Season with salt and pepper to taste. Sprinkle with the parsley.

● This easy favourite with limitless possibilities is equally at home with a simple baked chicken, a delicate Naturschnitzel, or meat.

——— ••• ———

BROCCOLI TIMBALE

FOR SIX PEOPLE

small knob of butter, plus
  butter for the dishes
700 g (1$\frac{1}{2}$ lbs) fresh broccoli
1 egg

6 tablespoons double cream
salt and freshly ground white
  pepper to taste
pinch of grated nutmeg

1 Preheat the oven to 170°C/325°F/gas 3. Butter six individual ovenproof dishes.

2 Cook the broccoli in boiling salted water until tender. Drain and purée in a blender or food processor with the egg, cream, and a small knob of butter. Season with salt, pepper, and nutmeg to taste.

3 Fill the dishes with the broccoli mousse. Place the dishes in a roasting tin and pour warm water into the tin until it comes halfway up the dishes. Cook in the oven for 50 minutes.

4 Serve as quickly as possible.

● A delicate, easy accompaniment for veal or seafood, it is wonderful served alone as a light vegetarian supper dish for two.

———— •••• ————

CHAMPAGNE CABBAGE

FOR SIX PEOPLE

85 g (3 oz) butter
2 medium onions, finely sliced
1 teaspoon caraway seeds
1 medium head white cabbage, rinsed, cored, and sliced into thin strips
1 teaspoon sugar

4 tablespoons white wine vinegar
225 ml (scant ½ pt) Champagne
8 tablespoons double cream
salt and freshly ground white pepper to taste

1 Melt 60 g (2 oz) of the butter in a large saucepan and sauté the onions and caraway seeds over medium-high heat for 4 to 5 minutes.

2 Add the cabbage slices and sauté for about 3 minutes.

3 Stir in the sugar. Add the vinegar and champagne. Bring to a boil and reduce until there is very little liquid left.

4 Stir in the cream, the remaining butter, and salt and pepper to taste.

5 Serve with the main dish or separately.

● In Viennese cuisine, this is a traditional accompaniment for poultry and game.

———— •••• ————

VIENNESE RED CABBAGE

FOR SIX PEOPLE

4 tablespoons vegetable oil
1 onion, finely sliced
1 medium head red cabbage,
   rinsed, cored, and sliced into
   thin strips
1 tablespoon sugar

225 ml (scant $\frac{1}{2}$ pt) red wine
1 bay leaf
$\frac{1}{2}$ stick cinnamon
salt and freshly ground white
   pepper to taste

1 Heat the oil in a large saucepan and sauté the onion over medium-high heat until golden.

2 Add the cabbage and sauté for 4 to 5 minutes, stirring occasionally.

3 Stir in the sugar and allow to caramelise.

4 Pour in the red wine, add the bay leaf and cinnamon, and cook until tender. Season with salt and pepper.

● To give this cabbage a special sweet-sharpness you can sprinkle in some tart berries after cooking.

———··———

GLAZED CUCUMBERS

FOR SIX PEOPLE

6 medium cucumbers
45 g (1$\frac{1}{2}$ oz) butter
6 tablespoons clear chicken
   stock or brown veal stock

2 tablespoons chopped fresh
   dill
2 teaspoons sherry vinegar
salt and freshly ground white
   pepper to taste

1 Peel the cucumbers, cut lengthways, remove the seeds, and cut into 1.25 cm ($\frac{1}{2}$″) slices.

2 Melt the butter in a frying pan. Add the cucumber slices, sauté for 4 to 5 minutes over medium-high heat, and add the stock. Simmer over low heat until the cucumber is tender but not too soft, about 5 minutes.

129

3 Stir in the dill and sherry vinegar, and season with salt and pepper to taste.

4 Serve as a side dish or on the plate with the main course.

———— •••• ————

CHICORY IN CREAM

FOR SIX PEOPLE

4 medium chicory, the cores removed, and cut into 2.5 cm (1")-thick slices
small knob of butter
4 shallots, peeled and finely diced

4 tablespoons double cream
juice of ½ lemon
salt and freshly ground white pepper to taste

1 Blanch the chicory in boiling salted water for 1 minute and then refresh in iced water.

2 Heat the butter in a frying pan, add the shallots, and cook over low heat for 4 to 5 minutes, without browning. Add the cream and reduce over low heat to a sauce consistency, about 5 minutes.

3 Add the chicory and lemon juice. Heat through and season with salt and pepper.

———— •••• ————

BRAISED FENNEL

FOR SIX PEOPLE

butter for the dish
3 medium heads fennel, cut in quarters lengthwise, then sliced at an angle into 2.5 cm (1")-thick strips

8 tablespoons brown veal stock
1 bay leaf
4–5 peppercorns

1 Preheat the oven to 180°C/350°F/gas 4. Butter an ovenproof dish.

2 Place the fennel in the dish. Pour in the stock. Add the bay leaf and peppercorns. Cover with aluminium foil and braise in the oven for 15 minutes.

3 Remove the fennel from its braising liquid and serve.

● This is particularly good with fish.

——— •••• ———

KOHLRABI GRATINÉ

FOR SIX PEOPLE

6 kohlrabi, each weighing 170 g (6 oz)
knob of butter, plus butter for the dish
8 tablespoons brown veal stock
4 tablespoons double cream
1 egg yolk
salt and freshly ground white pepper to taste
1 garlic clove, peeled

1 Peel the kohlrabi and cut into 2.5 cm (1")-thick slices.

2 Heat the butter in a frying pan and sauté the kohlrabi for 3 to 4 minutes. Add the veal stock and simmer, uncovered, until the kohlrabi is partially done, about 25 minutes.

3 Butter a gratin dish and preheat the grill.

4 Beat the cream and egg yolk together and add to the kohlrabi. Reduce over a low flame for 5 minutes, to a sauce consistency. Remove from the heat and season with salt and pepper to taste.

5 Add the garlic clove, return to a simmer, and cook for 3 to 4 minutes. Remove the garlic.

6 Remove from the heat and transfer to the gratin dish. Place under the grill until browned and bubbly. Serve in the gratin dish.

● The kohlrabi, a special turnip-like root vegetable much loved in Austria, is becoming more widely available. This dish goes particularly well with grilled meats.

CREAMED SPINACH

FOR SIX PEOPLE

1 kg (2 lb) spinach leaves,
   cleaned and the stems
   removed
170 ml (scant ⅓ pt) brown veal
   stock
½ garlic clove, peeled
small knob of butter

3 tablespoons flour
4 tablespoons double cream
salt and freshly ground white
   pepper to taste
¼ teaspoon grated nutmeg, or to
   taste

1 Blanch the spinach in boiling salted water for 2 to 3 minutes.
Drain.

2 Purée the spinach in a blender or food processor with the
veal stock and garlic.

3 Heat the butter in a frying pan. Remove from the heat and
stir in the flour to make a roux.

4 Stir the spinach purée into the roux. Return the frying pan
to the flame and stir in the cream, bring quickly to a boil, and
remove from the heat. Season with salt, pepper, and nutmeg
to taste.

● A traditional side dish for Tafelspitz, slowly simmered
beef.

———— ·•· ————

GREEN BEANS WITH BACON

FOR SIX PEOPLE

450 g (1 lb) green beans, rinsed,
   ends cut off
6 slices bacon

salt and freshly ground white
   pepper to taste

1 Boil the beans in salted water until still crisp and refresh in
iced water. Drain.

2 Make six bunches of the beans and wrap with the bacon. In a large frying pan, sauté the bacon-bean bundles for 2 to 3 minutes over a high flame.

3 Serve hot, sprinkled with salt and pepper.

———•••———

GREEN BEANS WITH DILL

FOR SIX PEOPLE

700 g (1½ lbs) green beans, tips removed
45 g (1½ oz) butter
4 shallots, peeled and finely diced.
4 tablespoons or more brown veal stock

6 tablespoons double cream
3 tablespoons chopped fresh dill
2 tablespoons red wine vinegar
salt and freshly ground white pepper to taste

1 Cut the beans into 1.25 cm (½″) pieces. Blanch in boiling salted water for 2 minutes. Refresh in iced water and set aside.

2 Heat the butter in a frying pan and sauté the shallots over medium-high heat for 3 to 4 minutes.

3 Add 4 tablespoons veal stock and the cream, bring to a boil, and reduce over low heat to a sauce consistency, about 5 minutes.

4 Add the beans and simmer until tender. You may need to add more veal stock occasionally to maintain a sauce consistency.

5 When the beans are tender, stir in the chopped dill and vinegar. Season with salt and pepper to taste.

● Veal stock and dill give the beans a rich and refreshing flavour. Delicious with meat or chicken.

———•••———

TOMATOES STUFFED WITH SPINACH

FOR SIX PEOPLE

knob of butter
800 g (1¾ lbs) spinach (leaves only), rinsed
salt and freshly ground white pepper to taste

pinch of grated nutmeg
1 clove garlic, peeled
3 large tomatoes
3 tablespoons beef stock

1 Preheat the oven to 180°C/350°F/gas 4.

2 Melt the butter in a frying pan over medium-high heat, add the spinach leaves, cover, and allow to cook for a minute. Season with salt, pepper, nutmeg to taste. Remove from the flame.

3 Spear the garlic clove on a kitchen fork and stir it through the spinach several times. Allow the spinach to cool.

4 Blanch the tomatoes in boiling water, refresh in iced water, and peel. Cut each tomato in half and scoop out the seeds.

5 Stuff the spinach into the tomato halves. Pour the beef stock onto a small baking tray and place the tomatoes on it. Heat through in the oven for 2 to 3 minutes.

● A vegetable dish for beef and pork.

———— •• ————

VEGETABLES PROVENÇALE

FOR SIX PEOPLE

small knob of butter
2 medium onions, thinly sliced
2 medium courgettes
1 medium aubergine, unpeeled
1 medium yellow squash

8 tablespoons brown veal stock or bouillon
salt and freshly ground white pepper to taste

1 Preheat the oven to 170°C/325°F/gas 3.

2 Heat the butter in a frying pan and sauté the onions over medium-high heat until soft but not browned.

3 Cut the remaining vegetables in 2.5 cm (1″)-thick rounds. Cut the aubergine rounds into eighths.

4 Layer the onions on the bottom of a medium-sized roasting tin. Alternate layers of the other vegetables for a colourful effect.

5 Pour in the stock, cover with aluminium foil, and cook in the oven for 40 minutes.

● This array of vegetables is spectacular served with red meats—beef, game, or lamb.

—— ·•· ——

COURGETTE TARTLETS

FOR SIX PEOPLE

450 g (1 lb) courgettes, cut into thin strips
1 teaspoon salt
butter for the tartlet tins or flan tin
60 g (2 oz) Emmenthal cheese, grated
2 eggs, beaten
1 clove garlic, peeled and crushed

pinch of oregano
salt and freshly ground white pepper to taste

SHORT CRUST PASTRY
150 g (5 oz) plain flour, sifted
$\frac{1}{2}$ teaspoon salt
70 g (2$\frac{1}{2}$ oz) chilled lard
2–3 teaspoons iced water

1 Stir the flour and salt together in a bowl. Using two knives or a pastry cutter, cut the lard into the dry mixture until the mixture resembles coarse breadcrumbs.

2 Sprinkle 1 teaspoon of the iced water over the surface and mix it in quickly with a fork. Add more water as needed until the pastry just holds together. Do not overmix. Form the pastry into a ball and use immediately, or wrap in plastic wrap and refrigerate until needed, up to 24 hours.

3 Place the courgettes in a bowl, sprinkle with salt, and set aside.

135

4 Preheat the oven to 190°C/375°F/gas 5.

5 Butter six round tartlet tins (5 cm (2″) diameter or one 22.5 cm (9″) flan tin.

6 Roll out the shortcrust pastry to 1.25 ($\frac{1}{4}$″) thick and use to line the tartlet tins or the flan tin, covering the bottom and sides completely. Prick the bottom and sides, then place some dried beans in each tin. Bake until the pastry is half cooked, about 10 minutes. Discard the beans and allow the pastry to cool.

7 Keep the oven at 190°C/375°F/gas 5.

8 Squeeze the water from the courgettes and place them in a bowl with the cheese. Add the eggs, garlic, oregano, and salt and pepper to taste. Mix well. Fill each tartlet tin or the flan ring to the top with the courgette mixture and bake for 12 to 15 minutes for tartlet tins, 25-30 minutes for a flan tin, until golden and crusty on top.

9 Remove the tartlets carefully from the tins and serve warm.

● This is our version of quiche and is excellent with poultry and game. The individual tartlets are a nice touch for presentation, or you can use one can flan tin. Served with a tomato salad and crisp white wine, this makes a terrific summer lunch.

CHAPTER 10

Desserts

IN 1683 the Turks abandoned a lengthy siege of Vienna, leaving behind their supply of coffee beans. Under the guidance of Georg Kolschitzky, a soldier of fortune familiar with Eastern ways, the Viennese were quickly initiated into the pleasures of a new beverage. The first Viennese coffee-house was opened on January 12, 1685, and a way of life was born. An institution in Vienna, the coffee-house is a salon away from home, a place for chatting with friends, for relaxing, undisturbed, for hours on end. Gossip is exchanged, problems pondered, all between sips of aromatic coffee. Many kinds are served, the most famous of which is Kaffee mit Schlag, strong coffee smothered with generous dollops of whipped cream.

Coffee in Vienna is seldom enjoyed without a sweet accompaniment. Ever since sugar became widely available in Europe in the early nineteenth century, Austrians have excelled in pastry making, raising it to an art form and a passion. Nowhere else in the world is there such a unique variety of cakes, pastries, strudels, and biscuits as in this dessert lover's paradise. Four o'clock in the afternoon signals a special ritual. A snowy cloth is spread, fine china set, and the table laden with an assortment of freshly baked treats. Desserts are the high point of every meal. Austrians can conceive of a dinner without a first course but never of a dinner with a sweet conclusion.

Here are some of our most sophisticated, luscious, and dazzling desserts. Many are surprisingly light and easy—no one need forgo the fabulous experience of a Viennese dessert.

A note to the cook: never use salted butter in our recipes. You will also want to keep lots of vanilla sugar at hand.

VANILLA SUGAR

1 kg (2 lbs) sugar   2 vanilla pods

1 Pour the sugar into a large jar that will hold it all. Stick in the vanilla pods so they are covered with sugar.

2 Cover tightly and wait at least one week before using.

——— •••• ———

PRALINE PARFAIT

FOR TWELVE PEOPLE

225 ml (scant $\frac{1}{2}$ pt) double cream   85 g (3 oz) granulated sugar
170 g (6 oz) plain chocolate   100 g (3$\frac{1}{2}$ oz) praline paste
3 eggs   3 tablespoons cognac or brandy

1 Whip the cream in a large, chilled metal bowl and set aside.

2 Melt the chocolate in a double saucepan and allow to cool slightly.

3 Meanwhile, combine the eggs and sugar in a bowl and beat until frothy. Beat in the praline paste and melted chocolate.

4 Stir the chocolate-praline mixture into the bowl of whipped cream. Mix in the cognac.

5 Line a 2 litre (3$\frac{1}{4}$ pt) earthenware terrine with greaseproof paper. Pour the mixture into the terrine and freeze. Before serving, unmould the parfait and slice it.

● No special equipment is needed for this ultimate frozen treat. It is simple to make and can be done a day or two in advance.

——— •••• ———

138

WARM CHOCOLATE ALMOND SOUFFLES
Mohr im Hemd

FOR EIGHT PEOPLE

60 g (2 oz) plain chocolate
60 g (2 oz) butter, softened, plus
   butter for the dishes
50 g (2¾ oz) granulated sugar
5 small eggs, separated, at room
   temperature

70 g (2½ oz) blanched almonds,
   ground
3½ tablespoons plain
   breadcrumbs
Chocolate sauce (recipe
   follows)
50 g (2¾ oz) caster sugar

1 Preheat the oven to 180°C/350°F/gas 4.

2 Melt the chocolate in a double saucepan. Allow to cool.

3 With an electric mixer, beat the butter and sugar in a very large bowl. Add the egg yolks and blend well.

4 Beat in the melted chocolate, then the ground almonds and breadcrumbs.

5 In a separate bowl, whisk the egg whites until stiff peaks form, and carefully fold them into the batter.

6 Butter eight individual ramekin dishes and dust with the caster sugar. Pour in the chocolate mixture. Place the dishes in a pan of hot water. Bake for 20–25 minutes, cover the cakes with aluminium foil, and bake 10 more minutes.

7 Serve warm with whipped cream and the following chocolate sauce.

● Pamper yourself and your guests with this rich and moist flourless confection. Serve it right from the oven in individual dishes. Top with the silky chocolate sauce that follows.

——— •••• ———

139

CHOCOLATE SAUCE

MAKES 450 ML ($\frac{3}{4}$ PT)

350 g (12 oz) plain chocolate
5 tablespoons sugar

8 tablespoons double cream

1 Melt the chocolate in a double saucepan.

2 Stir in the sugar.

3 Pour the double cream into a pan. Add the melted chocolate and bring quickly to a boil. Remove from the heat immediately.

● This intense dark chocolate sauce is also perfect over ice-cream and with many of our other desserts.

———— ·•· ————

SALZBURGER NOCKERLN

FOR FOUR TO SIX PEOPLE

20 g ($\frac{3}{4}$ oz) unsalted butter
4 teaspoons currant or grape
   jelly
whites of 9 large eggs, at room
   temperature

100 g ($3\frac{1}{2}$ oz) vanilla sugar
zest of $\frac{1}{2}$ lemon, grated
yolks of 4 eggs
4 tablespoons granulated sugar
70 g ($2\frac{1}{2}$ oz) plain flour, sifted

1 Preheat the oven to 230°C/450°F/gas 8.

2 Place four 22.5 cm (9″) oval gratin dishes (or one large oval ovenproof dish) on a baking sheet. Divide the butter and jelly between the individual dishes; if one large dish, smear the bottom with the butter and then with the jelly.

3 Combine the egg whites, vanilla sugar, and lemon zest in a large metal bowl. Beat with an electric mixer at high speed until stiff peaks form.

4 Beat the egg yolks with the granulated sugar. Gently fold the egg yolks and flour into the meringue. Use a spatula to place three large mounds of the mixture into each gratin dish. Smooth the surface of each and bake for 8 minutes, until puffed and golden.

140

5 Serve immediately. This is especially good with Vanilla Sauce, warm Chocolate Sauce or the following cold strawberry sauce.

● Golden peaks and gossamer clouds of meringue make this speciality named for Mozart's birthplace one of the most irrestible dessert soufflés in the world. An ethereal delight that should be served right from the oven.

——— •‚• ———

STRAWBERRY SAUCE

FOR SIX PEOPLE

300 g (10 oz) fresh or frozen strawberries
2 tablespoons caster sugar

1 teaspoon fresh lemon juice
dash of kirsch (optional)

1 Combine all the ingredients in a blender or food processor. Blend well.

2 This sauce can be refrigerated for several days.

——— •‚• ———

COTTAGE CHEESE SOUFFLÉ WITH STRAWBERRY SAUCE

FOR SIX PEOPLE

4 eggs, separated, at room temperature
3 tablespoons granulated sugar
zest of 1 lemon, grated
225 g (8 oz) cottage cheese

6 tablespoons caster sugar
2 tablespoons fresh lemon juice
butter for the soufflé dish
300 g (10 oz) strawberries, rinsed and hulled

1 Preheat the oven to 180°C/350°F/gas 4.

2 Combine the egg yolks, granulated sugar, and lemon zest in a bowl and beat until creamy. Press the cottage cheese through a fine sieve into the egg yolks and whisk until smooth.

3 In a separate bowl, whisk the egg whites, 4 tablespoons of the caster sugar, and the lemon juice to a stiff meringue. Carefully fold the meringue into the cottage cheese mixture.

4 Butter an oval soufflé dish and sprinkle with 1 tablespoon of the caster sugar. Pour in the soufflé mixture. Do not fill the dish higher than, 5mm ($\frac{1}{4}$″) below the rim, to allow rising. Place the soufflé dish in a roasting tin of warm water that comes halfway up the sides and bake for 35 minutes.

5 Meanwhile, purée the strawberries in a food processor, strain, and sweeten to taste with about 1 tablespoon caster sugar.

6 Place mounds of the soufflé on individual dessert plates and serve the strawberry sauce separately. You may also unmould the soufflé on one individual serving plate, surrounded by the sauce.

● Austrians love cottage cheese desserts, healthy, low in calories, and wonderfully delicious when sweetened. Accompanied by a fresh sauce of summer strawberries, this soufflé makes for an exciting dessert, perfect for a light conclusion to a meal.

TOPFENKNÖDEL
Cottage Cheese Dumplings

FOR SIX PEOPLE

150 g (5 oz) butter
½ tablespoon vanilla sugar
zest of ½ lemon, grated
juice of ½ lemon
300 g (10 oz) cottage cheese,
  pressed through a sieve

2 eggs
4 tablespoons fine semolina
pinch of salt
70 g (2½ oz) dry breadcrumbs
3½ tablespoons caster sugar

1 Melt 30 g (1 oz) of the butter and combine with the vanilla sugar, lemon zest, and lemon juice in a bowl. Beat until frothy. Add the sieved cottage cheese and the eggs, and beat until smooth. Beat in the semolina and refrigerate for an hour.

2 Bring 2 litres (3¼ pts) of water with a pinch of salt to a boil in a large saucepan. With an ice cream scoop, form 12 round dumplings. Drop them into the water and allow to simmer approximately 15 minutes. The dumplings will rise to the surface when done.

3 Meanwhile, in a sauté pan, melt the remaining butter and brown the breadcrumbs.

4 Remove the dumplings with a slotted spoon and drain them. Roll the dumplings in the breadcrumbs.

5 Serve two warm dumplings per person, sprinkled with caster sugar. The Topfenknödel may be accompanied by the following Plum Sauce.

———— ••• ————

PLUM SAUCE

MAKES 680 ML (1¼ PTS)

juice of 1 lemon
up to 225 g (8 oz) sugar,
  depending on the tartness of
  the plums

1 cinnamon stick about 7.5 cm
  (3″) long
2 to 4 whole cloves
1 kg (2 lbs) fresh, ripe plums,
  with stones removed

1 Bring 175 ml (a generous ¼ pt), the lemon juice, 150 g (5 oz) of the sugar, cinnamon stick, and cloves to a boil.

2 Add the plums and simmer, stirring constantly, until the skins are shrivelled, about 20 to 25 minutes. Add more sugar to taste, if necessary.

3 With a slotted spoon, remove the plums to a bowl. Reduce the remaining liquid by half, strain, and pour over the fruit.

4 Allow to cool, and refrigerate. Serve with the Topfenknödel (preceding recipe).

● You might also want to try this colourful sauce over vanilla ice-cream. Any leftover sauce can be frozen.

FRUCHTKNÖDEL
Fruit Dumplings

FOR SIX PEOPLE

85 g (3 oz) butter
pinch of salt
zest of $\frac{1}{2}$ lemon, grated
1 whole egg
1 egg yolk
700 g ($1\frac{1}{2}$ lbs) cottage cheese
3 tablespoon soured cream
1 tablespoon caster sugar
215 g ($7\frac{1}{2}$ oz) plain flour
12 plums, or 12 apricots, or 18
   large strawberries
12 cubes of sugar (optional)

FOR PLUM DUMPLINGS
3 tablespoons finely ground
   poppy seeds (you can use a
   mortar and pestle)
1 tablespoon caster sugar

FOR APRICOT DUMPLINGS
3 tablespoons cottage cheese
1 tablespoon caster sugar

FOR STRAWBERRY DUMPLINGS
70 g ($2\frac{1}{2}$ oz) toasted plain
   breadcrumbs
1 tablespoon caster sugar

1 In a bowl, combine the butter, salt, and lemon zest. Beat until fluffy. Add the whole egg and egg yolk, and continue to beat to blend. Beat in the cottage cheese, soured cream, and caster sugar. Add the flour slowly and beat until smooth. Allow the dough to rest for 30 minutes at room temperature.

2 Remove the stones from the plums or apricots. If the fruit is not very sweet, place 1 cube of sugar in the hollow left by the stone.

3 On a marble pastry board, roll out the dough 1.25 cm ($\frac{1}{2}$") thick. Using a pastry wheel, cut the dough into twelve 12.5 cm (5") squares. If you're using strawberries, make eighteen 7.5 cm (3") squares.

4 Place a piece of fruit, cut side down, on each circle of dough and pull the pastry up around the fruit. Seal by pinching the pastry together. (The dumplings can be prepared up to 3 hours ahead to this point. Refrigerate until ready to boil.)

5 Bring 2 litres ($3\frac{1}{2}$ pts) salted water to the boil. Add 8 dumplings and simmer until they rise to the top, approximately 15 minutes. Remove with a slotted spoon. Keep warm on a covered plate. Repeat with the remaining dumplings.

6 TO SERVE:

Plum dumplings: Sprinkle with the poppy seeds and caster sugar.

Apricot dumplings: Sprinkle with the cottage cheese, pressed through a sieve, and the caster sugar.

Strawberry dumplings: Roll in the toasted plain breadcrumbs and sprinkle with the caster sugar.

● Austrian dessert dumplings are made with apricots, strawberries, cherries, or plums. Apricots are particularly plentiful in Austria. In spring the Wachau region is breathtakingly beautiful with its flowering orchards, and in summer there is an abundance of golden, fragrant apricots to be used for making fine jams and desserts.

MILCHRAHMSTRUDEL
Warm Cottage Cheese and Cream Strudel

FOR TWELVE PEOPLE

butter for the tin
flour to dust cloth
60 g (2 oz) butter, melted
caster sugar
vanilla sauce

STRUDEL DOUGH
215 g (7½ oz) flour
¼ teaspoon salt
2 tablespoons vegetable oil,
plus oil for the dough
1 egg
OR 2 packets filo pastry and 8
tablespoons unsalted butter

FILLING
125 g (4½ oz) softened butter
115 g (4 oz) granulated sugar
4 eggs, separated, at room
temperature
225 g (8 oz) cottage cheese
425 ml (¾ pt) soured cream
4 tablspoons flour
zest of 1 lemon, grated
pinch of salt
4 tablespoons vanilla sugar
60 g (2 oz) sultanas

ROYAL TOPPING
225 ml (scant ½ pt) milk
2 whole eggs
3 tablespoons granulated sugar

1 For the dough, combine the flour and salt in a large bowl. With an electric beater, blend the 2 tablespoons oil, the egg, and 170 ml (generous ¼ pt) water. Combine the dry ingredients, mixing to a smooth paste.

2 Throw the mixture on a table surface and knead firmly for 4 to 5 minutes, until the dough no longer sticks to the surface.

3 Shape the dough into a round bread shape, smear thoroughly with oil, wrap in a cloth, and allow to rest for 20 minutes.

4 If you are using bought filo dough, melt the butter and set aside.

5 To prepare the filling, in a large bowl, beat the butter and granulated sugar with an electric beater.

6 Beat in the egg yolks, cottage cheese, and soured cream. Add the flour and continue beating for 1 minute. Whisk in the lemon zest and salt.

147

7 In a separate bowl, whisk the egg whites and vanilla sugar to a stiff meringue. Carefully fold the meringue into the cheese filling. Gently stir in the sultanas and set aside.

8 For the topping, blend the milk, eggs, and sugar, and set aside.

9 Preheat the oven to 200°C/400°F/gas 6 and grease a Swiss-roll tin with butter.

10 Place a tablecloth over a table, dust it with flour, and roll out the dough as thinly as possible over the cloth until it becomes a translucent rectangle, about 90 × 60 cm (3 × 2'). If uing bought filo dough, lay some of the sheets out in a single layer on the tablecloth to make a rectangle approximately 90 × 60 cm (3 × 2'), brush with some of the melted butter, and cover with another layer. Continue through both packets.

11 Cover the dough with the prepared filling, leaving a 2.5 cm (1") border on all four sides. Fold in the left and right sides of the dough, lift the cloth, then roll the dough in the tablecloth into a strudel shape.

12 Place the strudel in the prepared tin, brush with the 4 tablespoons melted butter, and bake for 10 minutes, until the strudel is crisp. Lower the oven to 180°C/350°F/gas 4. Spoon the topping over the strudel and cover the strudel with aluminium foil, pierced with several holes. Bake for 30 minutes.

13 Cut the strudel into portions and serve warm, sprinkled with caster sugar and accompanied by Vanilla Sauce.

● If you do not wish to make the strudel dough, you will need: 2 packets filo dough, 115 g (4 oz) butter.

———— •●• ————

VIENNESE CHERRY STRUDEL

FOR TWELVE PEOPLE

1 recipe strudel dough
85 g (3 oz) butter, plus butter for
the Swiss roll tin
plain dry breadcrumbs
700 g (1½ lbs) fresh, ripe
cherries, with stems and
stones removed
4 tablespoons granulated sugar
flour
caster sugar

1 Prepare the strudel dough according to the preceding recipe for Milchrahmstrudel, steps 1–3, or use prepared filo dough.

2 Preheat the oven to 190°C/375°F/gas 5 and butter a Swiss-roll tin.

3 Heat 60 g (2 oz) of the butter in a frying pan and brown the breadcrumbs over medium-high heat.

4 Place the stoned cherries in a bowl. Stir in the granulated sugar and breadcrumbs with the butter they were browned in.

5 Spread a tablecloth over a table (minimum size 90 × 60 cm (3 × 2')) and dust with flour. Roll out the dough, then carefully pull and stretch it until it becomes a translucent rectangle.

6 Spread the cherry mixture over the dough, leaving 2.5 cm (1") border on all sides. Fold in the left and right sides of the dough, lift the cloth, then roll the dough in the tablecloth into a strudel form.

7 Slide the strudel onto the Swiss-roll tin, curved into a horseshoe shape. Melt the remaining butter and brush the strudel with it. Bake for 20 to 30 minutes, until golden.

8 Allow to cool slightly before slicing. Sprinkle with caster sugar.

———··———

VIENNESE APPLE STRUDEL

FOR TWELVE PEOPLE

1 recipe strudel dough (see
  Index)
60 g (2 oz) butter, plus butter for
  the baking sheet
1.125 kg (2½ lbs) crisp red
  apples, peeled, cored, and
  sliced
dash of rum
100 g (3½ oz) sugar
1½–2 tablespoons cinnamon

juice of 1 lemon
70 g (2½ oz) plain dry
  breadcrumbs
170 g (6 oz) sultanas
60 g (2 oz) chopped walnuts
flour
clarified butter, melted
caster sugar
whipped cream

1 Prepare the strudel dough according to the recipe for Milch-rahmstrudel, steps 1–3, or use prepared filo pastry.

2 Preheat the oven to 200°C/400°F/gas 6 and butter a baking sheet.

3 Place the apples in a bowl, combine them with the rum, sugar, cinnamon, and lemon juice.

4 In a frying pan brown the breadcrumbs in the butter over medium-high heat and combine with the apples, sultanas, and nuts.

5 Spread a tablecloth over a table (minimum size 90 × 60 (3 × 2′)) and dust with flour. Roll out the dough, then carefully pull and stretch it until it becomes a translucent rectangle.

6 Spread the dough with the apple mixture, leaving a 2.5 cm (1″) border free on all sides. Fold in the left and right sides of the dough, lift the cloth, then roll the dough in the tablecloth into a strudel form.

7 Slide the strudel onto the baking sheet, curved into a horse-shoe shape. Brush with the clarified butter and bake for 15 minutes, until golden.

8 Allow to cool slightly, slice, and serve with a sprinkling of caster sugar and whipped cream.

———— ·•· ————

BUCHTELN
Sweet Buns

FOR SIX PEOPLE

170 g (6 oz) strong plain flour
20 g (¾ oz) fresh yeast, or 3
   teaspoons dried yeast
3½ tablespoons sugar, plus 1
   teaspoon for the yeast
150 ml (¼ pt) lukewarm milk
60 g (2 oz) butter, melted, plus
   butter for the cake tin

2 egg yolks
zest of ½ lemon, grated
2 tablespoons white rum
pinch of salt
vanilla sauce (optional – recipe
   follows)
caster sugar (optional)

1 Sift the flour into a bowl and make a well in the centre. Crumble the fresh yeast into the well and sprinkle the yeast with a teaspoon of sugar. Add half of the lukewarm milk and stir it into the yeast with your finger until it reaches a sauce consistency. Do not stir in the flour. The yeast-milk mixture should form a puddle in the centre of the flour. Cover the bowl with a tea towel and keep in a warm place for 30 minutes. If using dried yeast, dissolve the sugar in the milk, sprinkle the yeast over the surface and leave until frothy.

2 If necessary, uncover the bowl, add the melted butter, the remaining milk or the milk/yeast liquid, the sugar, egg yolks, lemon zest, rum, and a pinch of salt. Work the dough with a wooden spoon until it no longer sticks to the side of the bowl. Cover again with a tea towel and leave until doubled in volume.

3 Preheat the oven to 200°C/400°F/gas 6 and butter a shallow, round cake tin.

4 Take the dough and with your hands form little round dumplings, each 1.25 cm (½″) in diameter. Starting at the centre of the tin, working outwards place the dumplings side by side. The Buchteln should just touch. Place the cake tin near the warm oven for about 25 minutes until well risen and then bake in the oven for 25 minutes, until the buns are brown and puffy.

5 Serve warm with the following Vanilla Sauce or with a light dusting of caster sugar.

● A dessert of Czechoslovakian origin that evokes memories of a warm country kitchen. For a comforting indulgence, try these puffy, rum-scented yeast rolls, bathed in the golden vanilla custard sauce that follows.

———— •••• ————

VANILLA SAUCE
Crème anglaise

MAKES 1.8 LITRES (2½ PTS)

5 egg yolks
125 g (4½ oz) granulated sugar
1.35 litres (scant 2 pts) milk

1 × 25 cm (10″) vanilla pod (or 2 shorter ones) or vanilla essence, to taste

1 Beat the egg yolks and sugar until frothy.

2 In a large saucepan, heat the milk to the boiling point, remove from the heat, and whisk in the egg yolk-sugar mixture.

3 Make an incision in the middle of the vanilla pods and scrape the inside of the pod into the pan. Add the pod and stir over very low heat for 5 minutes. Never allow the sauce to boil. If not using a vanilla pod, add vanilla essence to taste.

4 Strain the sauce and serve warm. Or allow to cool and refrigerate. This can be kept for up to a week.

———— •••• ————

MOUSSE AU CHOCOLAT

FOR EIGHT PEOPLE

450 g (1 lb) bitter chocolate
300 ml (½ pt) Vanilla Sauce
  (preceding recipe)

850 ml (1½ pts) double cream

1 Melt the chocolate in a double saucepan.

2 Allow the melted chocolate to cool slightly and whisk in the Vanilla Sauce. Cool to room temperature.

152

3 Whip the double cream. Fold the whipped cream into the chocolate-vanilla sauce mixture.

4 Distribute in individual dishes or a large oval dish and chill in the refrigerator.

——— ••• ———

Viennese Sweet Omelettes

Austrians do extraordinary things with sweet omelettes. For a difference, try these Viennese treats, impressive yet easy to make. Following a hearty soup, Austrians often make a supper of one of these magic transformations of eggs, flour, and milk.

——— ••• ———

KAISERSCHMARREN
Emperor's Whim

FOR FOUR TO SIX PEOPLE

150 g (5 oz) flour, sifted
225 ml (scant ½ pt) milk
4 tablespoons sugar
4 eggs, separated, at room
   temperature
2 tablespoons dark rum
zest of 1 lemon, grated
pinch of ground cinnamon
pinch of salt

45 g (1½ oz) clarified butter for
   cooking the batter
2 tablespoons sultanas
30 g (1 oz) butter
caster sugar (optional)
cranberry, apple, or pear
Compôte (optional – recipes
follow)

1 Preheat the oven to 180°C/350°F/gas 4.

2 Meanwhile, with an electric mixer, beat the flour, milk, and 1 tablespoon of the sugar to a smooth paste. Then beat in the egg yolks, rum, lemon zest, cinnamon, and salt.

3 In a separate bowl, whisk the egg whites and 1 tablespoon of the sugar to a stiff meringue. Carefully fold the meringue into the other mixture.

4 Over a medium-high flame, heat the clarified butter in each of two large frying pans, the second of which needs to be ovenproof – or use a flameproof gratin dish. Pour the batter into the first frying pan (it should be about 3.75 cm (1½″) deep) and cook on one side like an omelette, for about 10 minutes. Add the sultanas and flip the omelette into the second frying pan or gratin dish. Transfer the frying pan or gratin dish to the oven and bake for 10 minutes.

5 Remove the omelette from the pan or dish and, using 2 forks, tear the omelette into pieces. Return the torn omelette to the pan or dish and add the 2 tablespoons of butter and the remaining sugar. Cook over medium-heat, turning the pieces over, for 4 to 5 minutes, until caramelised.

6 Serve on four warm plates. Sprinkle with extra caster sugar, if liked.

● A light, crisp, rum-scented delight, studded with sultanas. Serve it the classic way with the fruit compôte recipes that follow.

—— ·•· ——

CRANBERRY COMPOTE

FOR FIVE TO SIX PEOPLE

450 g (1 lb) granulated sugar
225 ml (scant ½ pt) red wine

450 g (1 lb) cranberries, rinsed
and drained

1 Combine the sugar and red wine in a casserole. Bring to a boil and allow to simmer, uncovered, for 15 minutes.

2 Add the cranberries and simmer, uncovered, for 10 minutes, stirring occasionally.

3 Allow to cool and refrigerate until ready to serve. (This will keep up to a week.)

APPLE COMPOTE

FOR FOUR TO SIX PEOPLE

juice of 1 lemon
1 kg (2 lb) tart apples, peeled,
   cored, cut into quarters and
   then into eighths

100 g (3½ oz) sugar
1 fresh vanilla pod
zest of 1 lemon, grated
2–4 whole cloves

1 Combine 425 ml (¾ pt) water and the lemon juice in a casserole. Add the apples as you cut them up. Sprinkle with the sugar.

2 Stir in the vanilla pod, lemon zest, and cloves. Bring to a boil and simmer, uncovered, until the apples are soft, about 20 to 30 minutes.

3 Remove the apples with a slotted spoon and place in a bowl.

4 Boil the liquid until it is reduced by half. Strain it and pour it over the apples.

5 Allow to cool and refrigerate. This keeps well for up to a week.

————— •••• —————

PEAR COMPOTE

FOR FOUR TO SIX PEOPLE

This may be prepared in the same way as the Apple Compôte (preceding recipe), substituting 1 kg (2 lbs) of pears for the apples and 225 ml (scant ½ pt) dry white wine for the same amount of water.

————— •••• —————

PFANNKUCHEN
Pancakes

FOR SIX PEOPLE

70 g (2½ oz) flour, sifted
6 tablespoons milk
2 tablespoons single cream
3 egg yolks
1 tablespoon vanilla sugar
pinch of salt

4 egg whites, at room
  temperature
clarified butter
170 g (6 oz) mixed firm berries,
  plus extra for decoration
caster sugar

1 Preheat the oven to 130°C/250°F/gas ½.

2 With an electric mixer, beat the flour, milk, single cream, egg yolks, half the vanilla sugar, and a pinch of salt to a smooth consistency.

3 In a separate bowl, whisk the egg whites and remaining vanilla sugar to a stiff meringue. Fold the meringue carefully into the first mixture.

4 Heat a little clarified butter in a 15 cm (6″) preferably non-stick frying pan over medium-high heat. Scatter 2 tablespoons of the berries, sufficient for 1 omelette over the bottom of the pan. Cover with one sixth of the batter, to a height of 1.25 cm (½″). When browned, flip over and brown on the other side. Remove and keep warm in the oven while preparing the remaining omelettes.

5 Garnish the Pfannkuchen with more berries and a sprinkling of caster sugar. Serve with vanilla sauce.

——— ·•· ———

PALATSCHINKEN
Crêpes

MAKES 12 CRÊPES; FOR SIX PEOPLE

250 g (9 oz) flour (or more)
225 ml (scant ½ pt) milk (or
  more)
2 teaspoons caster sugar

pinch of salt
3 eggs
vegetable oil for frying the
  crêpes

1 Whisk the flour, milk, sugar, and salt till smooth. You might need to add a little more flour or milk for smoothness. Then whisk in the eggs.

2 Heat a little oil in a medium sized pan preferably non-stick, over medium-high heat and start the first crêpe by pouring in 4 tablespoons of batter. Allow to brown slightly, turn, and brown on the other side. Remove and continue making the individual crêpes, stacking them as they are ready. Keep warm on a covered plate, Add more oil as necessary.

3 Use these basic crêpes to prepare any of the next four recipes.

● Palatschinken are Austro-Hungarian crêpes. They are served with a variety of exciting fillings.

————— •••— —————

KAPUZINER PALATSCHINKEN

FOR SIX PEOPLE

200 g (7 oz) unsweetened
  chestnut purée
4 tablespoons double cream
6 tablespoons vanilla sugar
juice of 1 lemon

12 Palatschinken (preceding
  recipe)
knob of butter, melted
butter for the dish
chocolate sauce (see Index)
whipped cream

1 Preheat the oven to 180°C/350°F/gas 4.

2 Press the chestnut purée through a sieve into a bowl and mix it with the cream, vanilla sugar, and lemon juice. Spread 2 to 3 tablespoons of the mixture on the prepared crêpes.

3 Fold the crêpes in half, then fold again, bringing one corner over to the other corner to form a triangle, and brush with melted butter. Place in a buttered ovenproof dish and warm for 1 to 2 minutes in the oven.

4 Serve with chocolate sauce and whipped cream.

● This is our particular favourite – crêpes filled with a sumptuous chestnut purée, warmed in the oven and smothered with our dark chocolate sauce. If the chocolate sauce makes this dessert a bit too sinful for you, try it instead topped with vanilla ice-cream or freshly whipped cream sweetened with a little caster sugar.

— ••• —

TOPFENPALATSCHINKEN
Cottage Cheese Crêpes

FOR SIX PEOPLE

butter for the baking dish
12 Palatschinken (see above)
caster sugar
vanilla sauce

TOPPING
2 eggs
8 tablespoons milk
8 tablespoons buttermilk
3 tablespoons sugar

FILLING
115 g (4 oz) butter, softened, plus butter for the dish

zest of ½ lemon, grated
70 g (2½ oz) sugar
3 eggs, separated at room temperature
225 g (8 oz) cottage cheese, sieved
4 tablespoons buttermilk
pinch of salt
1 teaspoon vanilla sugar
juice of 1 lemon
45 g (1½ oz) sultanas
vanilla sauce

1 Preheat the oven to 200°C/400°F/gas 6, and butter a deep ovenproof dish.

2 Whisk all of the ingredients for the topping together and set aside.

3 For the filling, combine the softened butter and the lemon zest in a bowl, and beat until fluffy. Add the sugar, egg yolks, cottage cheese, and buttermilk and beat until frothy.

4 In a separate bowl, whisk the egg whites, salt and vanilla sugar. Add the lemon juice and whisk to a stiff meringue.

5 Carefully fold the meringue into the cottage cheese mixture and stir in the sultanas.

6 Cook the crêpes according to the Palatschinken recipe.

7 Spread 2 tablespoons of the filling mixture over each of the prepared crêpes and roll them. Place the filled crêpes in the ovenproof dish and cover with the prepared topping. Bake for 12 minutes, until golden.

8 Sprinkle with caster sugar and serve warm with vanilla sauce.

● These traditional Austrian favourites are filled with creamy, sweetened cottage cheese and baked with a golden dome of custard. A dream of a dessert served with warm vanilla sauce.

————— • • • —————

APRICOT PALATSCHINKEN

FOR FOUR TO EIGHT PEOPLE (2 CRÊPES PER PERSON)

60–115 g (2–4 oz) apricot jam, depending on number of crêpes
1–2 tablespoons dark rum, depending on number of crêpes
1–2 tablespoons cognac, depending on number of crêpes
Palatschinken (crêpes) (see above), as many or as few as you want
caster sugar

1 In a pan, over medium heat, warm the apricot jam with the rum and cognac.

2 Spread a generous tablespoon of the jam mixture over each crêpe and roll it up.

3 Serve with a sprinkling of caster sugar.

● This luscious golden treat is easy to prepare; just fill the basic crêpes with this glistening mixture of warm jam, rum, and cognac.

———— ·•· ————

Viennese Fried Fruits

Use the Palatschinken batter to make these simple and treasured Austrian desserts.

———— ·•· ————

SLICED APPLE FRITTERS

FOR SIX PEOPLE

6 tart apples, peeled, cored, and
  cut into finger-thick slices
3 tablespoons dark rum
juice of 1 lemon
3 tablespoons granulated sugar

1 teaspoon ground cinnamon
6 tablespoons oil for frying
1 recipe Palatschinken batter
caster sugar

1 Marinate the apples in a bowl with the rum, lemon juice, 3 tablespoons sugar, and cinnamon for about 10 minutes.

2 Preheat the oil in a frying pan to 180°C/360°F. (It will begin to crackle. Use a fat thermometer if you want to be sure.)

3 Draw the apple slices through the prepared batter and drip off the excess. Fry until golden brown.

4 Drain on kitchen paper and serve with a sprinkling of caster sugar.

● These fritters make a terrific dessert, but are splendid served with omelettes or scrambled eggs or juicy sausages. Strawberry Sauce makes a fine accompaniment when the fritters are served for dessert.

160

SCHLOSSERBUBEN

Apprentice Locksmiths – Fried Almond-stuffed Prunes

FOR SIX PEOPLE

36 prunes, stoned
36 blanched almonds
3 tablespoons dark rum
3 tablespoons granulated sugar
6 tablespoons oil for frying
1 recipe Palatschinken batter

60 g (2 oz) cocoa mixed with 1
 tablespoon sugar
caster sugar
vanilla sauce or chocolate
 sauce

1 Stuff each prune with 1 whole almond.

2 Marinate the prunes in the rum and 3 tablespoons sugar for 10 minutes.

3 Heat the oil in a frying pan to 180°C/360°F (it will begin to crackle). Draw the prunes through the batter and allow the excess to drain off. Fry until golden brown, about 2 minutes.

4 Drain the prunes on paper towels and roll them through the cocoa. Sprinkle with caster sugar and serve with vanilla or chocolate sauce.

—— ••• ——

SACHERTORTE

FOR SIXTEEN PEOPLE

125 g (4½ oz) butter
85 g (3 oz) caster sugar
6 eggs, separated, at room
 temperature
few drops vanilla essence
125 g (4½ oz) plain chocolate
¼ teaspoon salt
85 g (3 oz) granulated sugar

85 g (3 oz) flour, sifted
225 g (8 oz) apricot jam
whipped cream

GLAZE
225 g (8 oz) granulated sugar
250 g (9 oz) plain chocolate

1 Preheat the oven to 200°C/400°F/gas 6. In a large bowl, cream the butter and the caster sugar with an electric mixer. Beat in the egg yolks and the vanilla.

2 Melt the chocolate in a double saucepan. With the electric mixer, beat the melted chocolate into the butter-sugar-egg yolk mixture.

3 Beat the egg whites, salt, and granulated sugar to a stiff meringue. Slowly and carefully fold the meringue into the chocolate mixture. Re-sift the flour over the meringue mixture and gently fold in.

4 Line the bottom and sides of a 25 cm (10″) loose-bottomed cake tin with greaseproof paper. Pour in the cake mixture and bake for 45 minutes. Remove from the oven. Run a knife around the edge of the tin, reverse, and unmould onto a wire rack. Allow to cool.

5 When the cake has cooled, cut into two equal layers. Spread half of the apricot jam over one layer, cover with the other, and spread the rest of the jam over the top.

6 To make the glaze, place the sugar, 9 tablespoons cold water, and the chocolate in a pan over medium heat. Stir constantly until the sugar and chocolate have melted. Bring the glaze to 95°C/200°F/ on a sugar thermometer. Remove from the flame, stir with a spatula until smooth, and immediately pour over the top of the cake. The glaze will run down to cover the sides of the cake.

7 Let cool, slice, and serve with freshly whipped cream.

● One of the crowning glories of Viennese cuisine, Sachertorte is probably the best known and best loved of all our desserts. An earthly delight for the chocolate fancier, this cake was invented in 1832 by Franz Sacher, sixteen-year-old apprentice chef to Prince Metternich, the diplomat and enemy of Napoleon. Metternich was so enamoured of the cake that he served it the rest of his life. The dense chocolate cake, layered with apricot jam and covered with a gleaming dark chocolate glaze, won world renown for Sacher, who went on to found the most famous hotel and restaurant in all Vienna. The Sachertorte is a practical cake to make in advance, since it keeps for several weeks. Serve it in the approved Viennese way, accompanied by generous dollops of snowy whipped cream, a beautiful contrast with the dark chocolate glaze.

————— •.• —————

TOPFENSAHNETORTE
Viennese Cheesecake

FOR FOURTEEN PEOPLE

SHORTCRUST PASTRY BASE
85 g (3 oz) butter, plus butter for the cake tin
150 g (5 oz) flour, sifted
2 tablespoons caster sugar
1 tablespoon vanilla sugar
$\frac{1}{2}$ teaspoon salt
1 egg yolk

CAKE
3 eggs
zest of $\frac{1}{2}$ lemon, grated
juice of $\frac{1}{2}$ lemon
3 tablespoons granulated sugar
1$\frac{1}{2}$ teaspoons vanilla sugar
3 tablespoons flour

2 teaspoons cornflour
caster sugar

COTTAGE CHEESE FILLING
180 g (6 oz) cottage cheese
85 g (3 oz) sugar
pinch of salt
juice of 1 lemon
2 tablespoons vanilla sugar
2 egg yolks
300 ml ($\frac{1}{2}$ pt) double cream
3 tablespoons gelatine

FOR ASSEMBLING THE CAKE
3$\frac{1}{2}$ tablespoons apricot jam
caster sugar
seasonal fruit

1 For the pastry, preheat the oven to 180°C/350°F/gas 4, and butter a 25 cm (10") loose-bottomed cake tin.

2 Work the butter with the flour, caster sugar, vanilla sugar, salt, and egg yolk to make a dough.

3 Roll out the dough to fit the cake tin, prick several times with a fork, and bake until light golden, about 30 minutes. Remove and allow to cool.

4 For the cake, keep the oven to 180°C/350°F/gas 4, and line a 25 cm (10") loose-bottomed cake tin with greaseproof paper.

5 Beat the eggs, lemon zest, lemon juice, sugar, and vanilla sugar until frothy.

6 Sift the flour and cornflour together, slowly add the egg mixture, and work into a dough.

7 Fill the cake tin with the prepared dough and bake for 45 minutes.

8 Remove from the oven and sprinkle the top with caster sugar. Allow to cool, then invert on a large plate to unmould.

9 For the filling, press the cottage cheese through a sieve into a bowl. Add the sugar, salt, lemon juice, vanilla sugar, and egg yolks. Beat with an electric mixer until smooth.

10 In a separate bowl, whip the cream and set aside.

11 In a saucepan, soak the gelatine in 680 ml (1¼ pts) water and heat gently until dissolved. Slowly beat the gelatine into the cottage cheese mixture. Fold in the whipped cream.

12 To assemble the cheesecake, spread the apricot jam over the shortcrust pastry base.

13 Cut the cake into three layers. Place the first layer on the shortcrust pastry base, surround with a 25 cm (10″) cake ring and top with half of the cottage cheese. Finish with the last layer of cake and refrigerate for 30 minutes.

14 Remove the cake ring, sprinkle with caster sugar, and decorate with seasonal fruit.

● An incredibly light, creamy, and impressive cheesecake, perfect all the year round for dessert or coffee time. This cake may take some time, but then so do many good things in life.

————— ∙•∙ —————

LINZERTORTE

FOR TWELVE TO FOURTEEN PEOPLE

560 g (1¼ lbs) plain flour, sifted
450 g (1 lb) ground hazelnuts
450 g (1 lb) butter
600 g (1 lb 6 oz) caster sugar
1 whole egg

1 egg yolk, plus 1 egg yolk for
  glazing the cake
1 teaspoon ground cinnamon
zest of 1 lemon, grated
350 g (12 oz) blackcurrant jam

1 Preheat the oven to 180°C/350°F/gas 4 and butter a 30 cm (12″) loose-bottomed cake tin that is 5 cm (2″) high.

2 Work the flour, hazelnuts, butter, sugar, eggs, 1 egg yolk, cinnamon, and lemon zest to a dough.

3 Use your fingers to press a generous three quarters of the dough into the bottom and sides of the tin. Fill with the blackcurrant jam.

4 Roll out the remaining dough to 50 mm (bare ¼″) thick and cut into strips. Crisscross these over the filling. Beat the remaining egg yolk and brush it over the pastry. Bake for about 1½ hours, until cooked throughout. Allow to cool, and unmould.

●The mixture of ground nuts and flour has made the Linzertorte one of the best-loved Austrian desserts since it was first served in the early eighteenth century.

165

Chapter 11

Stocks

BROWN VEAL STOCK

MAKES ABOUT 3.25 LITRES (7 PTS)

4 tablespoons oil
1.8 kg (4 lbs) veal bones,
   chopped into 2.5 cm (1")
   pieces
115 g (4 oz) chopped vegetables
   (carrots, celery, celeriac)

70 g (2½ oz) chopped onion
70 g (2½ oz) tomato purée
425 ml (¾ pt) dry white wine
3 bay leaves
20 black peppercorns

1 Preheat the oven to 200°C/400°F/gas 6.

2 Heat the oil in a large roasting tin and sauté the bones over high heat until browned. Place the tin in the oven for 30 minutes. Return to the stove.

3 Add the vegetables and onion, sauté over medium-high heat for 5 minutes, and return to the oven for another 20 minutes.

4 Remove from the oven, add the tomato purée, sauté over medium-high heat for 5 minutes, and then add the white wine. Reduce in the oven for 30 minutes.

5 Transfer the contents of the tin to a large saucepan and add 6.5 litres (1¾ gals) water. Add the seasonings and simmer, covered, for 10 to 12 hours, slowly reducing the stock by half to 3.25 l (7 pts) of liquid. Skim the stock occasionally while simmering.

6 Strain the stock through a fine sieve lined with cheesecloth. Allow to cool, then refrigerate and remove the fat once it hardens.

●Brown veal stock is highly versatile and can be used successfully for all meat and game preparations. This

166

basic stock can be made in large quantities and stored in the freezer or refrigerator.

———— •• ————

BROWN GAME STOCK

MAKES ABOUT 3.25 LITRES (7 PTS)

4 tablespoons oil
1.8 kg (4 lbs) game bones, chopped in 2.5 cm (1″) pieces
115 g (4 oz) chopped vegetables (carrots, celery, celeriac)
70 g (2½ oz) chopped onion
80 g (2¾ oz) tomato purée

425 ml (¾ pt) red wine
225 ml (scant ½ pt) gin
1 bay leaf
20 black peppercorns
45 g (1½ oz) juniper berries (or 8 tablespoons gin)

1 Preheat the oven to 200°C/400°F/gas 6.

2 Heat the oil in a large roasting tin and sauté the bones over high heat until browned. Place in the oven for 30 minutes. Return to the stove.

3 Add the vegetables and onion, sauté over medium-high heat for 5 minutes, and return to the oven for 20 minutes.

4 Remove from the oven, add the tomato purée, sauté over medium-high heat for 5 more minutes, then add the red wine and gin. Reduce in the oven for 45 minutes.

5 Transfer the contents of the pan to a large saucepan. Add 6.5 litres (1¾ gals) of water, the seasonings, and the juniper berries. Simmer, covered, for 10 to 12 hours, skimming occasionally, until the stock is slowly reduced by half, to 3.25 litres (7 pts) of liquid.

6 Strain through a fine sieve lined with cheesecloth. Allow to cool, then refrigerate and remove the fat when hardened.

———— •• ————

BROWN BEEF STOCK

MAKES ABOUT 3.25 LITRES (7 PTS)

Prepare in the same way as Brown Veal Stock (preceding recipe), using 1.8 kg (4 lbs) beef bones instead of the veal bones.

For clear beef stock, used in soups, see Bouillon in Index.

———··———

CHICKEN STOCK

MAKES ABOUT 3.25 LITRES (7 PTS)

1.8 kg (4 lb) chicken bones, chopped
425 ml ($\frac{3}{4}$ pt) dry white wine
115 g (4 oz) chopped vegetables (carrot, celery, celeriac)

70 g ($2\frac{1}{2}$ oz) chopped onion
20 black peppercorns
3 bay leaves

1 Blanch the bones in boiling water for 5 minutes. Discard the water.

2 Place the bones in a large saucepan with 6.5 litres ($1\frac{3}{4}$ gals) cold water. Add the white wine and bring to a boil. Add the chopped vegetables, onion, and seasonings, and simmer the stock, uncovered, over medium-high heat, skimming occasionally, until reduced by half, about $1\frac{1}{2}$ to 2 hours.

3 Strain through a fine sieve lined with cheesecloth. Allow to cool, then refrigerate and remove the fat when hardened.

———··———

QUAIL OR PIGEON STOCK

MAKES ABOUT 3.25 LITRES (7 PTS)

Prepare like the Veal Stock (see above), substituting 1.8 kg (4 lbs) of the appropriate bones.

PORK STOCK

MAKES ABOUT 3.25 LITRES (7 PTS)

4 tablespoons oil
1.8 kg (4 lbs) pork bones,
   chopped into 2.5 cm (1″)
   pieces
115 g (4 oz) chopped vegetables
   (carrots, celery, celeriac)
70 g (2½ oz) chopped onion

3–4 garlic cloves, peeled
25 g (¾ oz) caraway seeds
80 g (2¾ oz) tomato purée
425 ml (¾ pt) dry white wine
20 black peppercorns
3 bay leaves

1 Preheat the oven to 200°C/400°F/gas 6.

2 Heat the oil in a large roasting tin and sauté the pork bones over high heat until browned. Transfer the tin to the oven for 30 minutes. Return to the stove.

3 Add the vegetables, onion, garlic, and caraway. Sauté over medium-high heat for 5 minutes and return to the oven for 20 minutes.

4 Remove from the oven, add the tomato purée, sauté for 5 more minutes, then add the white wine and seasonings. Reduce in the oven for 30 minutes.

5 Transfer the contents of the pan to a large saucepan and add water. Slowly simmer, covered, skimming occasionally, for 10 to 12 hours, until the stock is reduced by half, to 3.25 litres (7 pts) of liquid.

6 Strain through a fine sieve lined with cheesecloth. Allow to cool, then refrigerate and remove the fat when hardened.

———··———

LAMB STOCK

MAKES ABOUT 3.25 LITRES (7 PTS)

Prepare in the same way as Pork Stock (preceding recipe), substituting the appropriate bones, omitting the caraway, and adding a pinch of thyme when the stock is almost completely reduced.

169

FISH STOCK

MAKES ABOUT 3.25 LITRES (7 PTS)

Prepare in the same way as Chicken Stock (above), substituting the appropriate fish bones and heads.

Index